Unmuzzled

Also by Joe Bennett

Just Walking the Dogs (Hazard Press)
Sleeping Dogs and Other Lies (Hazard Press)
Fun Run and Other Oxymorons (Scribner UK)
So Help Me Dog (Hazard Press)
Sit (Hazard Press)
Bedside Lovers (and Other Goats) (Scribner UK)
Doggone (Hazard Press)
Barking (Hazard Press)
A Land of Two Halves (Simon & Schuster UK)

Unmuzzled

Joe Bennett

HAZARD PRESS
publishers

All the columns in this book were first published in
The Press, *The Dominion Post*, *Hawke's Bay Today*,
the *Otago Daily Times*, the *Waikato Times*
or the *Southland Times*.

First published 2004
© 2004 Joe Bennett

The author has asserted his moral rights in the work.

ISBN 1-877270-85-7

Published by Hazard Press
P.O. Box 2151, Christchurch, New Zealand
www.hazardpress.com

Cover design by G & A Nelson

Printed in New Zealand by Spectrum Print

Contents

Preface

All my previous books have had forewords. They weren't necessary. And nor, as it happens, were they forewords. My editor has just told me that they were actually prefaces.

So here is my first preface to be given its proper title. I am confident that it will prove every bit as enlightening as the forewords.

J.B.
Lyttelton
July 2004

How to be happy

Take your dog with you on holiday. Dogs love holidays and are good at them. They also love you and hate kennels. Furthermore, if you do take your dog with you, you will add to the sum of happiness in the world. And if those aren't reasons enough to convince you, then you are sick.

You don't have to wait for a dog to pack. A dog is always packed. It's got its collar on and it won't sulk if you forget the lead.

Dogs rarely throw up in the car. And if they do, they eat it back up. Nor do dogs squabble in the car. They just stick their heads out of the window and are happy. They like ice creams, but they don't whine for them. And they never ask if you're nearly there yet. Dogs think you're already there, because, for a dog, there is here, and here is the best possible place to be. In five minutes time the best possible place to be will be where you are in five minutes time. But dogs don't know that until they get there, because they have no command of the future tense.

Dogs don't mind if you go to the same place every year. Nor do they hanker for abroad in the belief that abroad is better. They don't imagine that if they go abroad they will somehow become more adventurous. A dog knows that wherever it goes it will just be the same old dog, and it is happy with that.

A dog doesn't ask if its bum looks big in this. A dog hasn't got a this for its bum to look big in. Nor has it got a big bum.

Dogs admire the way you barbecue. They will watch you barbecue for hours. If you burn all the meat you can hide it inside the dog. After the barbecue you can lay the cooled griddle on the ground. It will be clean in the morning.

Having a dog on holiday will excuse you from guided tours, craft galleries, souvenir shops and other places where you would spend money on stuff you don't want. Dogs don't want you to buy stuff you don't want. Dogs want you to play. Playing is better for you than buying stuff.

Because you have spent the year watching sport on television you will have forgotten how to play beach cricket. The dog will remind you. When you are trying very hard to win, the dog will pick up the ball and run into the sea. You will swear at the dog and chase it and then you will give up, stand still, look at the sky and laugh. Then you will say 'Thank you, dog, for reminding me how to play beach cricket.'

Dogs will help you meet people. Some people will say 'What a nice dog' and 'How old is your nice dog?' and 'What's your nice dog called?' These people are good people. If you are single you may have sex with some of these people. If you are not single, you can imagine having sex with all of these people. If you imagine having sex with them, the dog won't know. If you do have sex with them, the dog won't mind. Though it will want to join in.

You will also meet people who bunch their eyebrows and swear and say 'That dog should be on a lead'. These are sad people. They have become infected by fear and by the media and they have forgotten how to find happiness, and in particular how to find happiness in the happiness of others. Have nothing to do with these killjoys until after midnight. After midnight, go out and let their tents down. Take the dog with you.

When the killjoys are writhing and squealing under the canvas, the dog will think it's a game. Encourage the dog to join the game, then go back to your tent. The dog will come home eventually. The killjoys will go home in the morning. You can then move your tent to the killjoys' camping site because it is better than yours. The dog will be as happy in the new camping site as it was in the old camping site as it is in any camping site.

In sum, then, the best way to enjoy a holiday is to imitate your dog. Wear as little as possible. Presume people are nice until you find out otherwise. When something is going on, join in. When nothing is going on, sleep.

But it is hard to imitate a dog that isn't there. Take the dog with you. Everyone will be happy.

Lucy mon

Oh golly gosh, I'm having trouble with my eyboard. The letter ' '
seems to have got stuc.

I found this out when I sent an email to Andy and he wrote back
instanter saying 'What's a mon?' I wrote back saying 'mon' was a
form of address in Scotland, normally preceded, for reasons that
eluded me, by 'hoots'. 'Fair enough,' wrote Andy, 'but why are you
living the life of one?', which puzzled me a bit until I had a pee at
my previous email.

'Sorry,' I wrote immediately, 'having problems with the letter ' '.
Didn't mean mon, but rather mon, you now, one of those religious
chaps that lives in a convent', and Andy wrote back 'Don't you mean
monastery?' to which I replied, 'Not if he's a lucy mon, I don't.'

I touch-type of course. It would be unprofessional not to. But I loo
at the eyboard at the same time, because one can't be too sure in this
precarious world. Belt and braces, that's the way to go. And besides,
how else am I supposed to now where the letters are?

The consequence is, of course, that I don't loo at the screen, and I
fire off emails to Andy with no 's in them. As soon as he pointed out

the problem, I tried pressing the . I pressed it again and again and again. Once or twice it worked (see), but generally not a dicy bird.

In one way it was great fun. It threw up all sort of strangenesses that refreshed, I felt, the tired old language. 'Dicy bird', for example, brings to mind the great Condor of Fortune that once soared above the Andes. The Aztecs sacrificed ids to it in the hope that it would bless them with the shelter of its wings, instead of dumping on them from high in the sy.

And the missing ' ' breathed fresh life into old joes.

Patient: 'Doctor doctor, I thin I'm a leptomaniac.'

Doctor: 'Have you taen anything for it?'

The missing ' ' could have altered the course of history. 'iss me, Hardy,' says the dying Nelson, to which Hardy replies, 'Of course iss you. Who did you thin I thought it was?'

'No,' groans Nelson in extremis, 'I meant "iss me". Iss me now, Hardy, before it's too late. Please.'

'Shoot him, Lieutenant,' says Hardy. 'We can't let the crew see him lie this. He's gone completely boners.'

(Of course one can programme a computer to do fun stuff automatically. I sometimes amuse myself – it's a lonely life being a hac columnist – by telling the machine to replace the letter 'e' with something infantile like 'bottom' and then I typbottom a linbottom or two for fun, though I admit that it soon grows a bit tirbottomsombottom.)

Anyway, I suppose things could be worse. Imagine if I was writing a novel and I also lost the letter ' ', number four in the blooy alphabet, and I ha a main character in the novel whose name was ic. It would mae life very har inee.

I have got a 'd', fortunately, but the ' ' really has got stuc, and though, as I say, it is fun in one way, it is also disastrous. Because when I told Andy that I'd been living the life of a mon I was speaing the truth.

I've been monish because I'm writing a boo. It isn't a novel about Dic, but it is 85,000 words long and it's due at the publisher in four days. I'll get there, I thin, just, but it's been tough. I actually haven't had a drin for twenty-seven days, which is, I believe, the longest drought since about 1971. The liver thins it's in clover – though in four days time it's in for one hell of a shoc.

But with the polishing still to be done to the text I've now got a problem. It's all very well to write a column with no ' 's in it, but I can hardly whac this sort of thing off to the publisher. Should I just eep on eeping on, and try to sirt round all the words with ' 's in them, or should I try to fix the eyboard? And if I try to fix the eyboard, what if it all goes wrong and I only compound the problem. I've got this really trendy computer that won't tae a dis, so I can't mae a copy of the text. I could lose the lot. Six months wor up in smoe.

But I've got this little aerosol of stuff that advertises itself as 'the toolbox in a can' and perhaps if I just give the letter ' ' a teensy-weensy squirt, lie so

At the Dickens

I'd always wanted to get into motivational speaking but I owe the chance to my Auntie Debs. When she finally fell off the poop deck after a long and lucrative career in the fishing industry I was her sole heir. My brother got the cod.

But neither of us was interested in fishing. He sold his cod immediately and I palmed off my sole to a nice little man with a beard and a fork. We were rich. My brother was a born idler and took off for the land of milk and honey. But I stayed put.

For years, you see, I'd had my ear to the ground and my nose to the wind. As a result I had my eye on a struggling little motivational speakers' bureau in town. It was called the Dickens and had fallen on hard times.

On a breezy March morning I strode into the Dickens clutching my fishing cheque. I pushed open the battered door and found myself in a deep and fusty gloom. The place was scattered with dusty accoutrements. The Dickens was one bleak house.

As my pupils widened in the crepuscular office I made out a figure slumped over the only desk. I pulled out a gin bottle and he came to with a jerk. Pausing only to tell the jerk to beat it, I poured us both a stiff one and came straight to the point.

'Mr Dickens,' I said, 'I hear you got motivational speakers.'

He laughed a laugh so hollow that I tipped my slug of gin into it. 'Mate,' he said, 'I got more motivational speakers than you can shake a stick at.' He handed me a stick.

I shook it. And suddenly the dusty accoutrements took shape as human figures, shambling and derelict, score upon score of them. I tried to shake my stick at all of them but there were too many.

'How much for the lot?' I asked.

'Yours for a song.'

I gave him a Christmas carol and he was out the door of the Dickens before you could say knife.

'Knife,' said one of the shambling figures.

'Too late,' I said, 'he's gone. You're mine now. Now get out there and get motivating.'

'Ha,' said the shambling figure. 'You greenhorn. Any idea how many motivational speakers there are these days? The country's swarming with them. Ex-alcoholics, buggered triathletes, slimming champions, swimming champions, positive thinkers, stockmarket gurus – billions of us. And no one wants to hear us any more. People have seen through us. Everyone I know in the industry is trying to get out of it.'

Before you could say Jack Robinson I realised what I had to do. I buttonholed the shambling speaker. 'Name?' I barked.

'Jack Robinson,' he said.

'Jack,' I cried, 'we have nothing to fear but fear itself. I'm going to release your creative energies in a way that you wouldn't have dared to dream possible. Are you with me, Jack?'

'Whatever,' said Jack gloomily, 'but I never was into that positive thinking caper. I was the super-memory man. You know, twenty tapes for three easy payments of $99, guaranteed to help you recall everyone's name at a party.'

'Yeah, yeah,' I said, 'what happened to that racket?'

'Don't remember,' said Jack, 'but it's dead now, like everything else in this biz.'

'He's right,' came a voice, 'you don't have to be a rocket scientist to see it's all over, mate. They've rumbled us.'

'Name?'

'Kuzolski. Rocket scientist. Chief safety engineer on the Voyager mission.'

'The one they lost touch with?'

'No, the one that blew up 'cause of a cock-up by the chief safety engineer. When NASA gave me the elbow I thought I'd try the motivational speaking line. " 'Your mistakes are your biggest asset' by the man who blew up the space probe." Thought it would be a nice comfy little number, you know, regular pay cheque, no responsibilities, all that stuff. And look at me now. Look at all of us.' He gestured to his fellow motivators, slumped in the shadows. 'We're dog tucker, mate, yesterday's men. No one's swallowing our baloney any more. Unleash your creative potential, be the CEO of your self, every idea's a good idea.' He chuckled. 'That particular idea was probably the worst of the lot.'

A murmur of assent scurried through the ranks.

'So,' I said, 'if motivation's a goner, where do we go from here?'

'Demotivation?' said one wag, from the echoing depths of his gloom.

'Precisely,' I bellowed. 'Got it in one.' I sensed eyes flicker into life and look up at me.

'It's time,' I said, 'to rediscover the wisdom of the ancients. Delude yourself is out. Know thyself's back in.'

I looked at my congregation of demotivated motivators. An old familiar light was burning in their eyes. One by one their careworn faces were shaking off their looks of rusty depression and shining like new roofing iron. They were galvanised.

'Now, put your little thinking caps on. I want ideas. I want catch-phrases. I want mottos.'

'How about,' said Jack, ' "Dare to be ordinary"?'

'Be alive. Work nine to five.'

'Orville Wright was wrong.'

'Stay at work. You're just a jerk.'

I've no need to go on. You're familiar with the story. How the Dickens Academy of Demotivation blew the whole motivational speaker racket out the water. Made people happy to be who they were. Put all the team-building confidence courses into bankruptcy. To cut a long story short, I made a killing, cashed up at the peak of the market and flew out to join my bro in the land of milk and honey.

But things had turned sour for him. He'd come to a sticky end.

A cup of Eros

There are two things you should do with coffee: drink it, and give thanks for it.

And there are two things you shouldn't do with coffee: boil it and do research into it. For coffee is a good thing and there are few enough good things in this world and we should leave those good things alone.

But now some people have done research into coffee. I use the word research loosely, but not half so loosely as I use the word people. These people are intrusive, lab-coated, myopic, killjoy, thwarted pseudo-scientists. Some of them are necrophiles with bad breath. The rest are less appealing. I could, if pushed, be quite rude about these people.

These people did their research (and you just know that they pronounce research with the stress on the first syllable, which is as sure a sign of depravity as using a Walkman) and they came up with findings. Researchers never just find things. Instead they come up with things, in the manner of the extraordinary man who recently stuck his head under water for six minutes and came up with a world record.

When interviewed on television he said he felt ecstatic.

I don't know if the coffee researchers are capable of ecstasy. If they are I wouldn't like to see it. But I have seen the findings they came up with, and the nub of these is that coffee makes men, but not women, irritable.

Well, ha. It is seven in the morning. Beside me is a pint of coffee thick enough to hold the teaspoon upright. It is my second pint of the morning. And I am irritable. But to conclude from this scenario that the coffee caused the irritability is like concluding from a glimpse of a baboon that life in the jungle turns your buttocks purple.

The only reason I am irritated now, irritated to the point of incandescence, is that I have just read about this witless research.

I am not opposed to research. Research is merely curiosity, and curiosity will and should continue regardless of how many cats it kills.

But I am opposed to this particular research. I am not opposed to it because it makes women out to be more stable than men (though that, of course, is in tune with the ghastly zeitgeist), nor because it panders to a paranoia about what we eat and drink (though that, of course, is also in tune with the ghastly zeitgeist), but because its conclusion is wrong. It's as wrong as a Walkman. I can prove it. My evidence is me.

I run on coffee. I walk on coffee. I laugh on coffee. I play squash, chess and silly buggers on coffee. I am as addicted to coffee as I am to oxygen. And yet, as my dogs will verify, I am generally about as irritable as a nun on Prozac.

This research is simplistic nonsense. It implies that there are only two types of people, men and women. Drop a flat white into either, it suggests, and behold the consequences – a woman as serene as a floating wisp of summer cloud, a man so irritable that his buttocks turn purple.

The human being is a complex beast. Every ounce of serious research confirms this complexity. It confirms that the human brain is an underlit capital city and the researcher is a visually impaired tourist with a limp and no guidebook.

But not according to these researchers. For them the human being is as predictable as a slot machine. Into the man goes the caffeine and out of the man comes the irritability.

And as a result, say the researchers, men at work should refrain from coffee. It makes them less co-operative. Instead the men should cluster co-operatively round the gulping, farting water-cooler. Oh, spare us.

Has none of these researchers ever had a tough afternoon over his test-tubes, taken a break, poured himself a coffee, sipped at its muddy beauty, felt every muscle in his body sigh and expelled from between his hideously bearded lips a long slow aaaahhh of relief, releasing into the patient air every bitterness, every frustration, every ounce of that perilous stress-making stuff that weighs upon the heart? Presumably not. So he doesn't understand that coffee is magic. It is good and necessary magic, consoling magic in a spiky world.

And magic is perilous stuff. The researchers are fools to fiddle with it. For evidence I offer the myth of Psyche.

Psyche had a lover. His name was Eros. She did not know his name. He came to her every night after the sun had set and he left before it rose. In the intervening darkness he made love to her with an intensity that left her sighing with pleasure, radiant with pleasure, floppy with pleasure, as if, indeed, she'd just drunk three flat whites.

But pleasure wasn't enough for silly Psyche. One night she set a lamp beside her bed. When Eros came and did his stuff once more then fell asleep in her arms, she leant carefully across and lit the lamp so as to do research on her lover. A drop of hot oil fell on Eros's shoulder. He woke and he fled. And he never came back.

20

Good as a rich monk

A nice corporation rang me. They wanted me to write a little something for them. 'We'll pay you,' they said, '75 cents a word.'

I liked that. ($2.25.) I liked that a lot. ($3.75.) I liked that so much that a surge of liking rose within me, a tsunami of liking, towering tall and voluminous and green as greenbacks, then breaking warmly over me and receding to leave a mass of creamy suds of loveliness, knee-deep and swirling in my bank account.

Had that last sentence been written for the corporation, it would have been worth $34. That's more than fifteen times as valuable as the sentence 'I liked that', which says as much, and says it better. Although now that I've used 'I liked that' twice, its value has doubled. Well, actually, I've now used 'I liked that' three, no, four times, so it would have raked me in a total of $9. I've done jobs where I earned $9 an hour. Oh, I liked this job. I liked it a lot.

What a doddle. Fancy a coffee? Let me write you a coffee. There, I've written you one, the frothiest cappuccino. No, don't thank me. It was a pleasure. Want chocolate on the top? Or rather, would you like a little chocolate sprinkled on the top? There you go. At 75 cents a word that's all the chocolate you could possibly want.

To coin a phrase, I would be phrasing coins. This was money for jam, and even more money for a sugar-laden fruit preserve. To enrich it, and me, still further, I had only to add 75 cents worth of pectin. Or of arsenic. It's all the same to me. 'What's the value of words?' asks the man of action. 'Seventy-five cents each,' say I.

This had to be the only job in the world where 'seventy-five cents' was worth $2.25. And 'two dollars twenty-five' was worth $3. But 'three dollars' was worth a mere $1.50, which is only half the value of 'a mere dollar fifty'.

It felt like a form of magic. By typing 'dog food' I fed my dog. If I wanted to treat her to a dried pig's snout, of which she is inordinately fond, I had only to write a dried pig's snout into existence.

Here was the world inverted. The world is things. We gave the things names. Now I had only to name the things to earn them. For sure it would take a while to write myself a house, but not so long as it would take to build one.

And I liked the way that the length of the word didn't matter. For one thing, I had always thought that I was worth as much as that ghastly vamp Madonna. Now 'I' was. And for another thing, I prefer short words to long words. Long words are like cushions. Short ones are like fists.

And with this scheme I would quite rightly earn as much for 'gut' as I would for 'stomach', or for the even primmer, pseudo-medical 'abdomen'. I liked that. I liked that a lot. It gave me a good feeling in the gut.

But every silver lining, apart from being worth $1.50, brings a cloud. The cloud this offer brought was called inflation. Because I now understood, and grasped, and comprehended, the reason for that awful form of language so often found in corporate and bureaucratic worlds.

I've fumed, not to mention raved, and even fulminated, against such language many a time (and oft) but now it all came clear. Those corporate and bureaucratic boys and girls must be paid by the word.

How else to explain the substitution of 'at this moment in time' for 'now'. How else to justify the 'window of' that always serves to introduce a corporate opportunity.

The best prose is spare as a monk's cell. A single chair and table. Walls as blank as honesty. The sort of prose that Orwell wrote.

Such prose is ill rewarded. Orwell coughed himself to death on some Hebridean island. Writers should be paid, not for the words they write, but for the words they cross out. They never will be.

Meanwhile here was my invitation to the corporate boardroom, its armchairs stuffed with adjectives. Waiters simpering through the throng, one hand held deferentially behind the back, the other toting a laden tray of Latinate synonyms and rich adverbial modifiers. 'Take all you want,' says the host, urging me to gorge on the stuff that clogs the arteries of prose and stills the little beating heart of truth.

Orwell would have scoffed at the offer. I took it. Every man has his price, and mine is 75 cents a word.

I wrote the piece, doing my best to quell the urge to pad it. I sent it in. They turned it down. 'It might upset some customers,' they said.

How did I feel? I felt good. Good as a monk.

'But we'll still pay you for it,' they said.

How did I feel? I felt very good. Good as a rich monk.

It was, as I said, a very nice corporation.

Hapsburg staplers

'Everything's interesting,' I said.

'Everything?' she said.

'Everything,' I said. 'Lana Coc-Kroft, heavy metal, heavy petting, heavy water, diseased Peruvian conceptual artists, the lot.'

'Staplers,' she said.

'Well,' I said, 'perhaps not staplers, but Namibian cooking classes, phone-card collecting, Tahitian voting habits, the whole caboodle, every little bit of it is...'

'Staplers,' she said. 'You said that everything was interesting and everything includes staplers. So kindly explain why staplers are interesting. Come on. I'm waiting... No? I'm not surprised. Because staplers are just bureaucratic tools and bureaucracy is about as interesting as athlete's foot.'

'Which, interestingly,' I said, 'is most common among non-athletes.' But I might as well not have spoken.

'I mean,' she went on, 'what is bureaucracy but a doomed attempt to compartmentalise? Divide a random world into topics, assemble some pages on each topic, then clip them with the stapler and drop them into the file marked sussed. A futile business, doomed as the kakapo, but necessary to gratify the sort of tiny mind that cannot cope with lack of order. You can see it in the very way a man applies a staple, aligning the papers just so, angling the stapler at precisely 45°, then applying cautious pressure with the heel of his pudgy hand so that the scrap of metal passes through the wad without buckling and then neatly folds its arms on the other side, smug as the buddha under a tree, as if to say, that's done, that's dealt with. Next.

'And if, despite the man's precautions, the staple still insists on buckling and thus mars the perfect neatness of the whole, what does our deskbound functionary do but reach for his destapler, a baby pair of pincers designed specifically and solely for removing buckled staples without the risk of doing damage to the dirtless finger-nails of Wellington? It's all so petty and depressing, so lacking in breadth, vision, risk. So come on, tell me why staplers are of the least interest to anyone at all except a shallow-minded, raincoat-wearing bureaucrat.'

'Well,' I said.

'And you are not allowed,' she said, 'to refer to the way boys at school insist on opening staplers out and using them as guns.'

'I wouldn't have dreamed of mentioning it,' I said.

'Because,' she said, 'that is merely typical of the primitive male psyche that seeks to turn everything into a weapon without regard to its purpose or to the waste of natural resources. Boys scatter staples as they scatter sperm. It's violence and profligacy without thought, the hallmark of the male. And while we're at it, do you know what is the biggest trading commodity today on this faltering little planet of ours? Do you imagine it's wheat or oil or fertiliser or something similar?'

'Staplers?' I ventured.

'It's armaments, boyo,' she said, pronouncing the word as if it were checkmate, 'armaments. And who commissions the armaments, designs the armaments, makes the armaments, sells the armaments, buys the armaments and presses the little buttons that fire the armaments? Answer me that, sonny.'

'Men?' I said.

'Men,' she said. 'Men who were once boys and who ripped the staplers off their female classmates who were constructively assembling projects on solar power and vegetarianism, and then turned the staplers into guns, thus inverting the biblical injunction to beat swords into stationery.'

'Ploughshares.'

'Exactly,' she said, 'and now that you've mentioned it, where do you think staplers come from, eh? I'll tell you where they come from.'

'Oh good,' I said.

'No,' she said, 'bad. Ever seen a stapler factory? Of course you haven't. The prosperous self-indulgent west doesn't make staplers any more, or anything else that's useful. We've forgotten how to make anything except armaments and geopolitical gaffes. We hand over all the humdrum manufacturing to what we're fond of calling the under-developed countries, where they employ six-year-olds with rickets.'

'I see,' I said.

'Oh no you don't,' she said. 'You barely see the start of it. That's just...'

'No clichés, please.'

'The tip of the iceberg,' she said. 'Because in the humble stapler you can see the twenty-first century unfolding and the fate of the dominant culture. The west has become bureaucracy-laden, and over-intricate. It's the classic symptom of an empire in decline. It happened to the Hapsburgs, to the Romans and, for all we know, to the Incas. They all became stapler freaks.

'Right this minute power is shifting unstoppably east and south to the hungry busy places, places like India, Indonesia and the hugely menacing China, places where they're not ashamed to get their hands dirty even if it means making silly little staplers for the effete societies that they are about to overtake and overwhelm and crush. So don't go around trying to tell me that staplers are uninteresting.'

'Sorry,' I said.

Nannies and billies

Ladies, would you like to meet men? If not, I don't blame you. But if so, come with me. I'll show you men. I'll show you a place where, as in the goldfields of Otago in 1860, men outnumber women by ten to one.

And these men aren't grizzled old miners with waist-length beards of sofa stuffing, men who lean scenically on shovels so that other miners can take sepia photographs of them to fill the museums of the future. No, these men are paydirt. They're nice modern men who wash and who apply under-arm deodorant just as the advertisers tell them to, so that they smell of rainforest. (Though rainforests, in my experience, actually smell of rotting vegetation and snakes, anacondas in particular. Anacondas stink. If you don't believe me, toddle down to the reptile house at your local zoo and have a sniff.)

Anyway, the men are nice men, and they're in a nice place. It's no Amazon jungle, this place, nor is it a nineteenth-century goldfield with huts and water-races and camel-coloured mud that can suck a boot off. No, this place is fluorescently lit, temperature-controlled, clean as an operating theatre and full of men. And stuff.

All sorts of stuff. Mushrooms, buttons, button mushrooms, washing powder (in which rainforest flavour is also available, so you can make your wardrobe smell like your armpits) baked beans, string beans, Lima beans, bean sprouts, beans from Africa, beans for Africa. It's a supermarket, ladies, and it's packed with men.

You shouldn't be surprised. Did you think it mere coincidence that the word supermarket is an anagram of sperm-u-krate? Yes, so did I.

But what you probably want to know is which supermarket. Which of the many supermarkets in Christchurch is the sperm-u-krate, awash with rainforest lovers? I shall tell you. Are you listening closely now? Are you intent? Are you keen and focused like an anaconda that has just spotted a goat?

Well, if so, beware. Goats are not indigenous to rainforests. Most rainforest goats are actually bait laid by snake-hunting German zookeepers. The idea is that the anaconda swallows the goat whole then settles into a post-lunch stupor. An anaconda is no sprint champion at the best of times, but with a goat inside it it can barely crawl. So all Herr Zookeeper has to do is amble up in his scoutmaster shorts and drop the snake into a hessian sack. No need even to feed it, there being already a captive goat to sustain it on the long flight to Düsseldorf.

But anyway, the supermarket. It's Woolworths. The big new Wool-worths at Ferrymead. Go there at 8.30 on a Saturday morning and you'll find that the place is full of men. Bizarre but true. I've been there.

Last Saturday morning I watched the men. I didn't see a single shopping list. I didn't see a single dither. I didn't see a single man read a label or check for fat content. I saw only swift decisive movements, hunting raids, the bean tin seized and tossed into the trolley with the speed of a zookeeper bagging a snoozing snake. The trolley never stopped moving. These were men shopping with a purpose. That purpose was to finish shopping.

It was like Ruapuna with groceries. The more the men loaded the trolleys the faster they pushed them, partly because a loaded trolley corners better, but mainly because every item in the trolley meant they were one step nearer the chequered flag of the check out and then freedom.

It was lovely. No foot-tapping waits behind aisle-blocking conversationalists. No squeezing past a woman scanning thirty-seven brands of identical pasta. No wayward steering. Only a silent masculine camaraderie of haste.

At the checkout, there were two men in front of me. Neither man flicked through a magazine backwards. As the groceries passed over the beeperscope neither man checked the prices on the little screen. And neither man seemed surprised to be asked to pay for his groceries. Both, indeed, were not only ready to pay, they were eager to pay. And of course, but of course, neither man wrote a bloody cheque.

No, each man was already swiping his discount card through the slot even as the checkout girl was asking if he had one. And each man answered the eftpos question about whether he wanted cash, even before it could be asked.

And having done the financial stuff, each man was already in position at the driving bar of the trolley, and moving off, when the checkout girl handed him the printout in the manner of a relay runner passing the baton. It was all so swift and wonderful.

So ladies, if you want to find men, men in abundance, responsible domestic men, try Woolworths in Ferrymead on Saturday morning early. But do so terribly carefully. You see – and I can't think of a nice way of putting this – I suspect that the men are at the supermarket at that hour of the day because, love you as they do, you aren't. So if you were to turn up in numbers, I think they'd smell a goat.

Playing with god

'Are you saved?' he asked.

We are supposed to live and learn. And if there is one thing I have learned from living it is to ignore people who ask me if I'm saved. It's a poor question at the best of times, and this wasn't the best of times. I was playing the man at chess.

I've joined an internet chess club. It's lovely. At any hour I can press 'seek' on my computer. This sends a tug down one tiny filament of the world wide web and somewhere in cyberspace a chess enthusiast will tug back. It can be anyone from an idle Indonesian to a Lapp at a loose end. A virtual chessboard appears before the pair of us, we agree on the time limit of the game and we're away.

Sometimes your opponent sends you messages while you play: 'Greetings from Grimsville, Latvia' – that sort of thing. I reply with 'Lots of love from Lyttelton', and generally that's that. For chess is a consuming business. No more words are exchanged until someone's king lies prone, a bishop's dagger buried in its kidneys. Then the politely jubilant Latvian types 'Thanx, good game' and scuttles off to find a better one. But not so with this man. He blocked my opening pawn with a pawn, then asked me whether I was saved.

Chess is psychological. Distracting an opponent is good. Upsetting him is better.

'Didn't know that I was lost,' I typed, then nudged another pawn.

He moved his bishop, then 'Do you know Jesus?' he asked. I didn't like this man.

He wasn't really asking. Rather he was smugly implying not only that he was on first name terms with Jesus – no Mr Christ for him – and that he was therefore heading upstairs for an eternity of harps and strawberries, but also that he cared about me. He didn't care about me. He'd never met me and he never would. For all he knew I could be a computer. (Several chess computers lurk in cyberspace. I avoid them. They thrash me by never making mistakes. Playing a computer is like playing god.)

I shifted my knight. Out came his queen. Then 'Do you know Jesus?' he repeated.

'Who?' I typed.

That got him. His reply was instantaneous and curt. 'Go see *The Passion of the Christ*,' he wrote.

My clock was ticking. Time is as cruel in chess as in life. When the end is near and death crowds around your king, you can never regain seconds that you frittered when the game was young. Nor can you retract your errors. Every sin returns to bite you. The pawn you casually ceded at the start proves eighty-eight moves later to be just the piece you need to plug the gap through which the final mortal thrust is coming. In chess you pay. In chess there's no forgiveness. I pushed out a third pawn to threaten his bishop and stop my clock.

Then 'No,' I typed. 'I won't see *Passion of the Christ*. I've already seen a film by Mr Melville Gibson. It was called *Braveheart* and though I don't wish to seem rude, I thought, on balance, that it was perhaps the most appalling piece of cinematic trash that I have had the ill luck to lay eyes on in all my forty-seven years. It starred a cast of rural Scots in kilts, each with an aura of virtue that didn't quite tally with my experiences of Glasgow on a wet Wednesday in winter. Their rugged goodness, flinchless courage and porridge-fuelled honesty were underlined by panoramic shots of heather, lochs and glens and other barren tourist falsehoods underscored with bagpipes. Braveheart himself, a sort of Jesus character, made Mills and Boonish love on horseback to an authentic Scottish peasant wench from Santa Barbara whose thirteenth-century make-up never ran, not even when they carried on beneath a waterfall accompanied by an unseen orchestra of fifty sweeping violins.

'The English, on the other hand, all looked like gargoyles. The king was a snivelling paedophile, his soldiers torturers or rapists. The English never gathered in romantic heather, but rather in some dungeon underground where all was dank and treacherous. And obviously every time an Englishman appeared on screen the orchestra shut up.

'In short,' I typed, and by this time my fingers were thumping the keyboard, 'it was a lousy piece of propaganda, the corniest corn since cornflakes, and if you're suggesting that a film director capable of producing that sort of pap could...'

The computer made a noise. I looked up at the screen. 'Game over' it said. My opponent's queen was nestled beside my king and guarded by his bishop. The simplest shortest gambit in the book of chess. Fool's mate.

'Thanx, good game,' typed Mr Are-you-saved and went.

There are times you have to laugh. This was not one of those times. I pressed the button called 'seek'. I had a new opponent within seconds. 'Greetings from Düsseldorf,' he typed.

'Lots of love from Lyttelton,' I answered. 'Are you saved?'

You live and learn.

When your turangawaewae crumbles

For seven years the table stood on the deck. And for much of those seven years my dog stood on the table. From there she could watch the world pass by, and bark at it if it looked threatening.

The table was not an outdoor table. It was an indoor table that I had stolen from a former place of work. I stole it by accident but I kept it by design. I kept it because my dog liked it.

It was a ponderous thing that was never going to make it onto Antiques Roadshow. Its legs were not turned. Its top was an inch thick. Its joinery was crude. And it took seven years to die, seven years of rain and sun and frost and sometimes an inch or two of snow. The death was fun to watch, in a slow-fun way. The underside of the table top stayed the colour of timber. The topside turned the colour of a corpse. And ever so slowly, glacially slowly, the planks that made up the table top shrank and separated and began to buckle. Shortly before it died the table looked like greyly frozen sea.

My dog didn't mind. She continued to lie or sit or stand on it and bark at distant poodles.

Then a couple of months ago the table collapsed. I saw it happen.

My dog stood up on it to bark and the table underneath her tottered. One joint gave way. That threw the load onto the other joints. They yielded one by one in accelerating succession. The table folded in on itself. It went down like a camel kneeling. It was the moment towards which seven patient years of weather had led. It was the inevitable climax, the tipping point, the point at which the forces of construction lost and the chaotic world won. Here was entropy in action.

My dog was unimpressed by entropy in action. She jumped off the toppling table and ran to me for succour. Her turangawaewae had crumbled. We all need succour when our turangawaewae crumbles.

I left the heap of wooden rubble where it lay. I liked the anguished silent randomness of it. I liked the way it sat in distinction to the straight lines of house and deck. But I felt sorry for my dog. She needed a place to see the world from. So after a week I built her one.

I measured major pieces in the pile of rubble and sketched a design in my head and drove to the timber merchant's. It was a daunting place. The men there had trailers on their utes and could reverse them. And they spoke about wood in a dialect I didn't understand. But a man with shorts and forearms took pity on me and spoke in English and redesigned my table plan and sold me the timber I needed and several tools I probably didn't. They included an electric drill. I'd always wanted an electric drill, but never found the excuse to buy one.

In the showroom was an outdoor table. It cost less than I had spent.

I am no carpenter, but I made a frame and it was almost square. I nailed the planks of my table top onto it and they held firm. I cut four legs and turned the table top upside down and screwed three of the legs into place so that they stuck up like the legs of a dead cow in a river. I screwed brackets inside the legs to hold them firm as the man in shorts had told me to. I put more screws in than I needed to because the drill had been expensive.

It was a chore to keep swapping drill bit for screwdriver head, so I stopped drilling holes. I just leant on the drill and drove the screw home. If the screw heads protruded I tapped them in with a hammer.

The fourth leg was a problem. My legs were not quite the same length. Nor were their ends quite square because I didn't have a tool to square them with. I thought a bit and then I turned the table the right way up, slotted the fourth leg into the frame, adjusted it until it touched the ground then held it in place with a couple of short nails. I followed the nails with a dozen long screws. Or at least I meant to. After five screws the drill screamed and smoked and died. I substituted nails for the remaining screws. Great big nails.

I shook the table. It stood firm. I decided not to lay a spirit level on it. I stepped back from the table and admired it. The fourth leg was a little askew, but I didn't mind. It had an honest look. I coaxed my dog to climb onto the table. She obeyed with caution. Then she sat down on the table. I sat on it too. I put an arm around my dog. Together on our turangawaewae we looked out on the world, defying the silent forces of entropy, and ready to bark.

Groovy

Eminent broadcaster Paul Holmes has been described as 'groovy and dangerous' by eminent broadcaster Paul Holmes. The news made the front page of the exciting *Sunday Star Times* and was accompanied by a large photograph of Paul Holmes looking groovy and dangerous.

The story has aroused a passionate response from *Holmes* fans. Spokesman for the Amalgamated Paul Holmes Fan Clubs, a Mr Holmes, said that it was good to see Paul Holmes thriving again after a year that Paul Holmes himself has described as 'gruesome'.

Spokesman Holmes said that during the year there had been 'a lot of payback going on' and, he added, 'a sense of delight in Paul's discomfort'.

But with typical magnanimity, said Mr Holmes, Paul Holmes had 'forgiven and forgotten' the whole business.

When asked by the reporter what it was that he had forgiven and forgotten, Paul Holmes replied 'the cheeky ... I can't even bring myself to say it', thus confirming that he had forgotten it.

Evidence of Paul Holmes's return to grooviness and danger, said Mr Holmes, was the re-energised *Holmes* show. According to Paul

Holmes, continued Mr Holmes, *Holmes* was 'rating its socks off'.

It was when nobody asked Paul Holmes why *Holmes* had regained its sparkle, that Paul Holmes came out with the line that thrust Paul Holmes onto the exciting front page. 'Suddenly I'm popular again,' said Paul Holmes. 'I'm a little bit groovy and dangerous.'

When nobody asked Paul Holmes why he had failed in this instance to refer to himself in the third person as Paul, Paul Holmes passed the unasked question to his publicist Mr P. Holmes. Mr P. Holmes said he resented the criticism implicit in the unasked question. After so many years in broadcasting it was inevitable that Paul Holmes would make the occasional lapse into the first person, but in the context of his prolific output those lapses were few.

Mr P. Holmes drew a comparison between Paul Holmes and the prime minister whose use of the third person was becoming more assured as her time in office grew. He cited the prime minister's reference to herself as a popular and successful prime minister. Admittedly, said Mr P. Holmes, the prime minister wasn't groovy or dangerous, nor was she rating her socks off at present, indeed she was barely unfurling a blue stocking top, but he was confident that, like Paul Holmes, she would regain success and popularity.

When a reporter didn't ask whether Paul Holmes had heard of Narcissus, publicist Holmes replied with a sneer that actually he preferred nail-clippers, but anyway the question was trivial. What mattered was the groovy and dangerous Paul Holmes and his incomparable list of achievements. 'The list includes,' began Mr P. Holmes, 'fronting a long-running and top-rating television show called *Holmes*, intruding on private distress, patronising the young and the weak, pandering to public taste, being spectacularly sycophantic to anyone associated with show business…' and here Mr P. Holmes interrupted his recitation to praise Paul Holmes's recent performance at the Oscar ceremony during which Paul Holmes described a Hollywood starlet in terms that would have been the envy of Elizabeth I's most obsequious courtier. 'It was broadcasting at its best,' said Mr P. Holmes the publicist, 'and evidence that Paul Holmes is returning to mid-season form. But Paul Holmes's achievements are not limited to broad-casting. He has appeared on I don't know how many women's magazine covers ("But I do," quipped Paul Holmes), undergone a helicopter crash, contracted a disease, and above and beyond this remarkable catalogue he has achieved…' but unfortunately the list of Paul Holmes's other achievements was drowned by a passing gnat.

When not pressed by a journalist to repeat the list, publicist Holmes refused on the grounds that Paul Holmes was a modest man who did not court publicity. But Mr P. Holmes advised anyone who sought the unbiased truth to consult Paul Holmes's autobiography published a few years ago with a picture of Paul Holmes on the front, and on the back a picture of Paul Holmes. It was called *Holmes*, said Mr P. Holmes, and it contained some spectacular use of the third person by Paul Holmes about Paul Holmes. Mr P. Holmes's own particular favourite was '… the turbulent world of the restless Paul Holmes was about to experience a seismic upheaval again'. The passage referred to an extramarital romance in which, contrary to rumour, only one of the parties was called Holmes.

Mr P. Holmes also referred to Paul Holmes's tantrums which, according to Paul Holmes, 'became legendary'. For evidence Mr P. Holmes quoted again from *Holmes* by Paul Holmes. 'One morning when I did something badly, I kicked a two-bar heater in the studio and it stayed there dented, for several years.'

It must be remembered, said Mr P. Holmes in summary, that in the world of current affairs there are no constants except the people who present current affairs. 'Paul Holmes,' said Mr P. Holmes, 'is a current affair. Well done, the *Sunday Star Times*.'

The root of things

Here's a story. Identify the moral, please, summarise it on the back of a postcard in not more than twenty words and post it to someone else. Because I'm off morals. 'Morals,' as the New York Jewish friend I haven't got didn't put it, 'schmorals'.

Things happen to happen. Their point is their pointlessness. Moral stories awash with poetic justice are just things we feed children in the hope of deluding them that the world's the right way up. Moral stories are pacifiers. The babies can suck and suck on them but they'll get none of the good milk of truth.

The story. My mate rang to say he should have died. The blowpipe, he said, almost killed him.

He's a fat vet. When I knew him at university he was neither of those things, but he was already galloping in their direction. At exam time he would stay up late with *The Anatomy of the Horse* and a couple of saddle bags of chocolate biscuits. In the morning *The Anatomy of the Horse* would still be there.

He now lives in Florida. When he met me there at the airport last year I made to hug him and got a third of the way round.

At university he also had a car, and it was equally clear where he was heading with that. He was destined for the book of sad statistics. It wasn't that he drove badly. He just forgot that he was driving. If he had a passenger he would find the conversation a greater attraction than the petty business of steering. If he didn't have a passenger he would often fall asleep.

He has crashed a lot of cars. In the footwell on the passenger side of every one of them you could see the worn carpet where his friends had repeatedly stamped on a brake they didn't have, and that he did have but was forgetting to use.

So far, obviously, he has survived his crashes. Perhaps his fat has acted as an airbag. I hope it continues to do so because he's a good kind man.

Anyway, he recently went to Malaysia for his roots. He was born there but left when he was four. He duly found his roots and hated them. He discovered he had been born into privilege, the colonial British enclave that appropriated all the nice bits of Kuala Lumpur for itself and kept servants. So he gave up on his roots and went looking for Malaysia's. He found them in a national park. Inside that park were long-houses full of Malaysian forest people. It sounds as voyeuristically horrible as all cultural tourism, but he says it was nice. He stayed a day or two in a long-house and got on well with his hosts. Presumably he didn't take them for a drive. When he left they gave him a blowpipe, as one does, and a pretty set of darts.

For the flight home he packed the darts in his suitcase but the blowpipe was too long so he carried it on to the plane, or tried to.

'What's that?' said the authorities.

'It's a blowpipe,' he said. He doesn't do dishonesty, which is why people like him and why he's a good vet. Animals trust him even when he's killing them.

'Ah ha,' said the authorities. And in these paranoia-laced times one can understand their ah ha. They would have had immediate visions of the Malaysian Air Accident Inspectorate picking over the smoking remains of a jet in the jungle and finding the charred corpses of pilot, co-pilot and purser each with a piece of Malay Air cutlery embedded in the back of the neck, so deeply embedded that it must have been projected at high velocity. Yet the voice recorder had registered no noise of explosives, only a sort of breathy whirr.

There would be an inquiry. The inquiry would eventually reach security.

'A blowpipe?'

'Yes. But he said the darts were in his check-in luggage.'

At the same time the story illustrates the intractable bovine stupidity of all rule-bound authorities. My friend is fat. There has never been a fat terrorist. And it would be a remarkable fat terrorist who tried to board a plane while openly carrying a metre-long Neolithic murder weapon.

Anyway the authorities wanted the blowpipe, but so did my mate. He demanded to see the supervisor. By the time the supervisor had come and then gone again to find the supersupervisor, the bird had flown. My mate caught the next plane, complete with blowpipe.

Driving home from Miami airport he fell asleep at the wheel and wrote his car off. He blamed exhaustion following the battle of the blowpipe.

And the moral? Well, I'll save you the trouble. Character is destiny. None of us changes much. But there's little mileage in knowing that. More useful perhaps is the suggestion that if you cheat death you should ring your friends. They'll be pleased to hear from you. It will reaffirm the fib they were told as children, that the world is the right way up.

Let's make with the jam

Jet-skiers. I've thought about them. I really have. I've even tried, and I know it's unfashionable, to be fair. But I can see no way around my original conclusion. They should be arrested. They should be convicted. And then they should have their nostrils packed with raspberry jam and they should be strapped to the ground in an area popular with soldier ants.

At the toe-end of a hot day my dog often takes me to the beach. She likes it there. She can frolic in the cool water and she can piss on the sandcastles that the kiddiwinkies have made and then forgotten. When she pisses, the crenellations darken then melt. And she can bark at seagulls. They don't seem to mind being barked at. They just do a bit of effortless wheeling and mewing then settle twenty yards up the beach, which is simply too far for my ageing dog to bother to amble for another dose of barking pleasure.

I like the beach too but I don't bark at the gulls and I never piss on the sandcastles until after dark. What I like is the Wordsworthian stuff.

Wordsworth wrote a sonnet about an evening on the beach. He

43

gave it an imaginative title. He called it 'Evening on the Beach'. Here's the start of it.

It is a beauteous evening, calm and free;
The holy time is quiet as a nun
Breathless with adoration; the broad sun
Is sinking down in its tranquillity.

The trouble with stuff like that is that you can't dislodge it. It enters your head at an early age and just sits there waiting. Thirty years later you pop down to the evening beach with the dog for a bit of pissing and communion, and the sea is calm and the air is warm and the sun is setting and the hills are darkening and a little flotilla of yachts is streaming across the bay, their sails as taut and sweet as pregnancies, and the ripples are susurrating on the sand and there's a great freight of peacefulness and you go, 'Oooh that's nice'.

And you try to decide exactly what it is that's nice about it, and your brain goes riffling through the memory banks as if they were some vast telephone directory. But instead of coming up with a startling new verbal arrangement that defines the relationship between the human and the sweetness of the great inane, the brain takes the easy route and comes up with Wordsworth. 'Holy time,' says the brain, 'quiet as a nun, and all that. There you go, that's that dealt with and pinned down. Anything else you want of me right now? No? Good, let's bugger off to the pub.' Which we did.

The following day the nor-wester blew and you could have grown rubber plants in my armpits, and the dog retired to the shade beneath the table on the deck, panting like a pump. But in the evening the wind abated and life was possible once more, and the dog and I went down to the seas again to the lonely sea and the sky, and all we asked was more of the same – sandcastles, gulls and nun-quiet. We got a jet-ski.

It was driven, astonishingly, by an adult. Less astonishingly he was a he. He drove in circles. In creative moments he drove in figures of eight. His jet-ski made a wake and then he drove excitingly over the wake. Physically he was going nowhere. Morally he was going backwards. He was reverting to infancy. He was a tot on a plastic tricycle making chugging noises. Here was movement for the sake of movement, power for the sake of power, noise for the sake of noise. Here was unthinking purposeless man driven by a grossly throaty engine and his own primordial testosterone.

The noise his contraption made had all the charm of a dental drill. The holy time was no longer quiet as a nun. The nuns were still breathless, but only because they were running away. And there, hot-footing it after them, was Wordsworth, his hands to his ears and the tails of his frock-coat streaming out behind him. And there was I, standing on the beach, cursing. Unlike the nuns, who are too nice, and Wordsworth who's too dead, I'd have happily hit the man. He had committed an act of theft. He had stolen the quiet, stolen the peace, plucked the necessary goodness from the evening and left only the bitter husk of anger.

Compare his contraption with the ancient silence of the yachts on the previous evening. On second thoughts, don't bother. The conclusions are too obvious. And anyway, now's not the time for thinking. I've done all that. Now's the time for action. Let's make with the nostrils and the raspberry jam. And a smear or two on the genitals might be amusing too.

Dear Mummy

Dear Mummy,

Thanks awfully for the jam roly-poly and the deep-fried pork pie. Good to know that English cuisine is still going strong, though it might be an idea next time to put them in separate parcels.

Unfortunately there were bits of your letter I couldn't decipher, but I managed to lick most of the jam off the long paragraph about the weather. What a hot summer you seem to have had! Cedric must be very excited about his tan. Exactly which part of his forearm is it on? Good to learn, too, of his success in the brewing business. Please convey my congratulations on his bronze medal in the beer-warming competition.

Talking of competitions, there's one going on down this way that you may not have heard of. It's called the Rugby World Cup. It lasts for about six weeks. For the first month or so, the half dozen countries in the world that take the game seriously, have a lot of fun bashing up the countries that don't. Then they bash each other up.

It's coming to an end now, and you'll be pleased to hear that the English chaps are doing jolly well. They've reached the final. But some awfully puzzling stuff has happened along the way.

For a start there's the New Zealand coach. I can't understand a word he says. Remember that gipsy woman who used to grab your arm at the tube station and run a grimy finger over your palm? Well, this coach comes out with exactly the same sort of mystical mumbo-jumbo, though at least he doesn't try to sell you a sprig of the lucky heather that he's bought in bulk from the garden centre.

Still, he was everyone's darling while his team was knocking up 300 points a time against Guernsey and the Tunisian under nineteens. And when they reached the semi-finals, the local Sunday rag biffed the television newsreaders off the front page for once, and replaced them with a photo of the team under the headline 'Semi-Gods'. Precisely one week later the team lost and the headline read 'World Chumps'. You have to feel sorry for them.

Even more puzzling was the man I heard on the radio this morning. He is the big boss of the national rugby club, but I think he's rather confused. When the interviewer asked him about the defeat, he said, 'The brand has taken a bit of a dent.' What can he have meant?

I know you don't know much about rugby, Mummy, but in essence it's like old-fashioned war. The secret is to drive your enemy back. I learned all about that in old Rocky Rockingham's history classes. He told us how the Duke of Wellington always believed in advancing hard, on the principle that it was dashed difficult for Johnny Foreigner to mount a cavalry charge when his horses were back-pedalling. Old Rocky used to demonstrate this by getting all the weedy boys with glasses or foreign mothers to stand up, and then telling the rest of us to pelt the weeds with pencils, shoes and geometrical instruments. With Rocky roaring encouragement, we'd soon have the misfits huddled in a corner of the room blubbering. It's the sort of lesson a chap never forgets. Old Rocky certainly knew how to teach. (I was sorry, by the way, to read in the last issue of the old school mag that he's finally tossed in his chalk. I was going to send a few lines of condolence to Mrs Rockingham, but then I thought back a bit and decided there probably wasn't a Mrs Rockingham. Anyway, rest his bones.)

But, as I say, rugby's a lot like that. Drive the other chaps back and the battle's more or less won, which is exactly what happened in the semi-finals. The Aussies did the Duke of Wellington stuff, and New Zealand soon became the gibbering misfits, all penned in the corner with quivering knees and runny noses and praying for the bell.

Apart from one fluke, the Aussies didn't score any of the pretty things they call tries, but everyone here quite rightly acknowledged that they'd played terribly well. They'd outsmarted and outbeefed the locals, and jolly good on them.

The following day the English boys – and honestly, Mummy, they are an ugly lot of bruisers – went out and did exactly the same thing to the French. The French were supposed to be all flair and intuition, but after an hour of bombardment from the uglies in white, flair and intuition looked like fifteen piglets in a very small slaughterhouse, all running into each other, squealing and terrified. The final whistle was a kindness.

And what did we get then? All hail to the conquering heroes? Cry God for England, Harry and St George? Not on your nelly, we didn't. All we got was a chorus of 'Oh, the boring Poms', led by the monocular old bats they wheel in to commentate.

And that's another thing, Mummy. Everyone, including the television newsreaders, is happy to call us Poms. No one calls the French Frogs, even though it was only a few years ago that they were sauntering round these parts merrily blowing up ships and atolls. Everyone hates us, Mummy. I don't pretend to understand.

But it's all a lot of fun. Wrap up warm for summer.

Lots of love,

Joe

Warm, wet and threatless

I had a theory about the bathroom habits of the sexes, but I lacked evidence to support it. So I went to the trouble and expense of doing a survey. With full statistical rigour I surveyed everybody sitting at the bar.

The survey resoundingly proved my theory to be true: women prefer baths and men prefer showers. Or, to put it another way, my survey confirmed that men are more sensible than women, more hygienic, thrifty, musical and conscious of the dwindling of the earth's resources. I enjoyed typing that sentence. It will bring me death threats.

My theory may also explain why men are still in charge of most things. By the time a woman has run a bath, got the temperature right, soaked herself, soaped herself and played with her duck, a man has had a shower, put on a tie, gone to work and done at least half an hour of shouting. But what it doesn't explain is why women like baths so much.

The bath has a totemic quality. It often appears in television advertisements, containing a lot of bubbles and a woman stupefied with pleasure. That woman is not me.

Nevertheless I was brought up with a bath. I was dropped into it every second night along with my elder brother. And it was in that bath I learned that there is no sensation worse than water up the nostrils. It spells panic in capital letters. I was also suspicious of shampoo. It tasted bad and stung the eyes, so God alone knew what it was doing to my hair. Now I know that too. It was making my hair fall out.

When my brother decided he preferred to bath alone – a decision forced on him by the courses he chose at university – I had to run my own bath. I soon learned that the perfect temperature for a bath is the one it isn't at.

I also learned that the hand is a bad thermometer. Dangle it in a too-hot bath and it will tell you that it's not too hot, so you step in. Feet are better thermometers, but they are slow. You can stand there for several seconds while the too-hot message lumbers up the legs, circumnavigates the pelvis, dawdles up the spinal column and then emerges through the oesophagus as a yelp. You leap from the bath like a pole vaulter and find you've gained a pair of vermilion ankle socks.

So you cool the bath a little, before stepping back in. Then you grip the sides and lower your vulnerabilities towards the water in the manner of a tentative anglepoise lamp.

At this stage you hold your breath, so that at the moment of contact you can emit a series of little gasps like a chimp's orgasm. As you finally submerge your shoulders and the water sloshes lovingly onto the bathroom floor, you complete the chimp orgasm with a long satisfied 'aaaah'.

But then what? A chimp just says thanks, cleans itself up and goes about its business. But the bath-taker, well, what is there to for him to do? Lie there stewing in his own dirt? Constantly and inaccurately adjust the taps with his toes in an effort to keep the temperature right?

Read a book? I've no idea. You'll have to ask a woman.

The only bath I remember liking was after rugby. Someone else filled it and both teams got into it. If you were the fifth team playing on a muddy day, the bath looked like a tourist attraction in Rotorua. But unlike a tourist attraction in Rotorua, you could smoke, drink beer and boast to twenty-nine other men in it.

These days I rarely bath with twenty-nine men. The last person I bathed with was Jane Austen. I'd bought a house that came with a salmon pink spa-bath studded with water jets in what looked like amusing locations. Eager to try it I plucked Jane from the shelves and stripped off. To make the jets jet there was a small electric motor conveniently housed just below my right shoulder. When I pressed the button to start it my eyes vibrated. So did Jane Austen. Sadly the eyes and Jane vibrated at different speeds. I gave up, got out and have never had a bath since.

But every woman I know has. Though showers are better than baths for all purposes, up to and including sex and opera, women persist in taking baths.

Why is this so? Relentless in pursuit of truth I put the question to all the women in my bar survey. 'What exactly is it,' I said to her, 'that you like about baths? Is it that they offer a refuge from a spiky world, a cocooning warmth and privacy, an escape from the demands of children and men? Or is it that you are fundamentally a tactile being and a bath is like a million warm and threatless hands exploring you? Or is it something Freudian, a journey of nostalgia to the womb, a floating in the waters of security, a reversion to an amniotic world?'

'Yeah,' she said. So now you know.

And we had another beer

He was seventy years old, in the pub, wearing a rib-knit fisherman's jersey and smoking a pipe, three-quarters of which was fine by me. And in the end I even forgave the jersey.

But it was the pipe I liked best. I rarely see pipes now. Soon I won't see them at all. Indeed I half-expected to make out a museum curator hovering in the gloom between the pokies and the pool table, waiting for Pipeman to go suddenly pasty, clutch at his chest, slide from the bar stool, describe a startled pain-driven pirouette, collapse, twitch twice and cark it. At which point Mr Museum would scuttle from the shadows, slip the corpse into a curatorial body-bag and lug it with the strength of his excitement to his publicly funded basement. There his assistants with their white coats, austere hair and surgical gloves would suck out Pipeman's fluids, fill him with formalin, buff him up a bit, insert the pipe between his wire-strengthened fingers and mount him in a glass case for the edification of tomorrow's bored school parties. He would be a central exhibit in a diorama called Twentieth-century Folly. Next door would be a parallel display called Twenty-first-century Enlightenment. It would feature a lycra-wrapped bimbette with cheek bones, breast implants and a grin like a wedge of Gouda, frozen in the act of running on a treadmill while injecting herself with vitamins, listening through earphones to a motivational CD and studying company accounts on a laptop clipped to the handlebars. All this before a background of the gym crèche, where the mum-deserted tinies would be learning how to slide a condom over a banana.

But if there was a curator in the pub that evening, he trudged home disappointed. Pipeman was hale and busy. What kept him busy was his pipe. He used his little pipeman's penknife to scrape the bowl. Then he tapped the charred bits into the big glass ashtray. Then he unfurled his pipeman's pouch, extracted a moist wad of baccy, tamped it into the bowl with his square-ended pipeman's thumb, rasped a non-safety match into life, tilted it till the flame crept half an inch up the stem, put the pipe to his lips, held the match over the bowl and sucked. He sucked three, four times, then exhaled approximately 70 cubic feet and growing of a fragrance so redolent of wood, walnuts, molasses and contentment that I nearly swooned. Then he took a swig of beer, laid the pipe in the ashtray and let it go out. It was lovely, and I said so.

And Grant and I spent an hour talking to Pipeman.

He had married, fathered a brood, worked in something white collar for a long long time and accreted a house full of things. One by one his brood grew up and flew the nest. Then his wife died. Then his work ended. And he was left all alone in his house with a pipe.

So he sold the house and bought a boat. And though his children disapproved – oh, spare us all from disapproving children – he went to live in it. He sails it a bit, but most of the time he doesn't. He potters about and mends it and paints it and sits in it to read and think. At night he likes the whisper of the water on the hull. And he is neither lonely nor alone. Around him, he said, there are several other solitary ageing men on boats. They say hello to each other. Sometimes they get together. More often they don't.

I didn't ask him if he was happy. It's a poor question. And anyway I didn't have to.

Soon the barmaid announced that his meal was ready and Pipeman picked up his pipe and said good evening and went to the dining room. Grant and I sat in silence for a while. And then we spoke at the same time, and I said, 'Go on, you first.' Grant said that Pipeman reminded him of a time when he was twenty-one in London and had just bought a rusty old campervan and was setting out for Europe with no ties, no duties and no reason to do anything but go and be.

I nodded.

'And you?' said Grant.

I said that he reminded me of hitchhiking in winter on the edge of the Canadian Prairies. It was sunny but well below zero. And the land was so flat I could see a car approaching for fifteen minutes before it reached me. There was little traffic. Indeed there was nothing but snow and sky and me. A dot appeared in the distance. I watched it swell into a blue car. When it was perhaps 600 yards away I put out a gloved thumb. A hundred yards short of me it slowed down. And then as it drew closer still I put my thumb back in my pocket. The puzzled driver crawled past me, then drove away. I watched his car turn back into a dot, leaving me alone and tiny and free between snow and sky. And I felt good.

'Yes,' said Grant, and we had another beer.

Lies to spare

Lies hold our world up. Take away the scaffolding of lies and things fall down. God, pornography, 100 per cent Pure New Zealand, deodorant, down they tumble. Rubble the lot. It's great fun.

Take mega-butch four-wheel drive recreational vehicles. I wish you would. I can't see round them, past them or under them. Monstrous things, rolling off the automated assembly lines in Nagoya and Seoul, to infest the world. They're built of lies, lies from here to my Aunt Fanny. Lies from bull bar (Oh, those poor shunted bulls. You have to go miles these days to find an unshunted one) to tailgate.

Let's look at the tailgate. I often have to. It blocks my windscreen. It's got a spare wheel stuck on it.

Small cars haven't got a spare wheel stuck on them. Minis find space for their spare wheels somewhere inside. Mega-butches don't. Though their cabin space is measured in hectares, there's no room for the spare.

A lie, of course. There's room to spare for the spare. But the spare is hung on the back for a reason. It's hung there to tell fibs. 'Look at me,' bellows the spare, 'I am rugged practicality. My owners wear safari suits with sweat stains in the armpits. My owners know the world's awash with peril. My owners can cope.'

The dangling spare tyre implies that the moment one of the other tyres is picked off by a sniper, or holed by an assegai, or shredded by a landmine in the badland wastes of the supermarket carpark, Mr or Mrs Safari-Armpit will leap from the cab, fall to their knees on the sun-bleached tarmac and make with the jack before you can say charging rhinoceros. They are rugged and practical people, men and women of action, terse, hard and with honest dirt beneath their fingernails. So says the spare.

But that isn't all it says. The spare tyre is shrouded in a tyre cover. That tyre cover prompts a question. That question is why?

The tyre cover can't be there to keep the tyre dry. Tyres don't mind getting wet.

And the tyre cover can't be there to protect the hands and clothing of Mr and Mrs Safari-Armpit. These are rugged people who care nothing for a smudge of dirt on the safari suit.

No, that tyre cover exists to send yet another lie out into the world to breed. The one I pootled along behind today told me a corker of a fib. And all in three words.

The first of these words was the name of the car-maker. Let's call it Carcorp. The other two words, in sequence, were 'likes' and 'nature'.

Carcorp likes nature. Well, isn't that just dandy.

Let's start with the first lie. Carcorp doesn't like nature. Carcorp doesn't like anything. It doesn't like cricket or pavlova or sex. It can't. It isn't a sentient being. It doesn't have feelings.

Carcorp is an organisation of lots of sentient beings, some of whom may like cricket, pavlova and sex, some of whom may even like them simultaneously, and some of whom may like none of them. But the only thing that binds these beings together is not what they like and dislike, but the making and selling of cars in order to earn dosh. Which is fine by me. I approve of cars. But not of fibs.

The purpose of saying 'Carcorp Likes Nature' is that we then think of Carcorp as a person, and a nice person at that. Carcorp is not going to publish a slogan such as 'Carcorp Kills Cats', even though it's a chunky, alliterative and memorable slogan. And a true one. Worldwide in the course of a normal day Carcorp probably runs over several tonnes of cats. But cat-slaughtering doesn't make Carcorp out to be a nice chap. No, Carcorp likes nature.

Nature here means cuddly things. It means soft grass and lapping waters and gentle herbivorous beasties that feed from our hands and look good on postcards.

If 'Carcorp Likes Nature' is true, then, by the rules of logic, the following statements must also be true. Carcorp likes blowflies. Carcorp likes warthogs. Carcorp likes death from exposure. Carcorp is particularly fond of that remarkable Amazonian parasite that a bloke told me about in the Volcano last week so it must be true. This parasite can swim up a stream of urine, take a grip, wriggle into the urethra and, well, you can imagine the rest, but I'd advise you not to.

Carcorp is lying. Spectacularly. Mr and Mrs Safari-Armpit buy Carcorp's cars because nature is nasty. Carcorp's cars shelter them from its brute indifference. Carcorp's cars ford rivers, scale scree, flatten saplings and pollute the world, while Mr and Mrs Safari-Armpit sit in air-conditioned comfort listening to Vivaldi.

None of this matters, of course. Carcorp's slogan is no worse than ads for toilet-tissue happiness or deodorant-driven sex, but it does seem to me to be a neat irony, that a company whose products are the brilliant inventions of scientific human reasoning should need to use emotional lies to sell them.

A betting man

When Jono Gibbes was a first year at secondary school he laid a bet. He bet a friend a thousand dollars that he would become an All Black.

When I was a first year at secondary school I, too, laid a bet. I bet Dave Collier a thousand pounds that we would never reach the senior year at school.

Mr Gibbes's bet was based on his ability at rugby. My bet was based on Hammersley. Hammersley was head prefect. As far as I knew he didn't have a Christian name. Nor did he need one. Hammersley was plenty.

I saw and heard him for the first time on stage in a school assembly. He had a voice like the fat string on a cello. He also had sideburns. From 20 yards away those sideburns looked like possums. From 10 yards away you could see them growing.

There were seven years between me and Hammersley, and a mountain range called puberty which I couldn't imagine ever crossing. Hammersley was a man.

By being a man Hammersley belonged to a group that included teachers. Teachers were less impressive than Hammersley. Their teeth were the colour of tobacco and so were their jackets. Those jackets had leather patches on the elbows. Some of the teachers had herbicidal halitosis. The rest had homicidal halitosis. And most of the teachers sagged. Hammersley didn't sag. He bristled. Nevertheless both teachers and Hammersley were men.

So were fathers. Some fathers bristled, others sagged, but most were just remote figures. My own had been born in the First World War and fought in the second. Not surprisingly, he never mentioned the former, but neither did he mention the latter. He seemed to have no past. He was, I think, a kind man and a good one, but to me he seemed distant, a member of that unthinkable adult tribe that I could not imagine joining.

In theory, of course, I knew that I had to become a man, but in practice I couldn't believe it. Men were a different species. When I looked at Hammersley or teachers or my father, I felt as caterpillars must feel when they see butterflies.

What made men so different was their apparent lack of emotions. Principal among these was fear. Men were never frightened. If something had threatened Hammersley, he would have merely sprouted another sideburn, sounded a bass note on the cello and sent the enemy scuttling.

We did see occasional frightened teachers. Dave Collier got under the skin of one man until he shook. When he wrote on the board the straight lines looked like the printout from a seismograph. He didn't last long. I hope they found him a nice bed. But the existence of such weaklings actually confirmed me in my belief that some males never made it to manhood.

The only emotion that proper men displayed was anger. Anger was rare, volcanic and dangerous, but you could see it coming. The mountain started to glow and pulse and spit gouts of lava, and then it was time for children to retreat.

Last weekend Jono Gibbes played for the All Blacks and finally won his bet. And thirty years ago I reached the last year at school and lost mine. Shortly afterwards an article appeared in the school magazine. I can quote one line of it exactly. It came from a collection of first impressions of new pupils at the school. 'And then we lined up for dinner,' wrote one eleven-year-old, 'and we were prodded by prefects and they were enormous, just like men.' He was writing about us, about Dave Collier and me.

I don't know if Jono Gibbes has received his thousand smackers, but I never paid Dave Collier his. This was partly because I didn't have the money, and partly because Dave forgot. But mainly because I've never felt that I actually lost. Though the first years saw us as men, I didn't. And I still don't. I am now well over twice the age of the sideburned Hammersley. My father's dead and I'm five years older than he was when I was born. I'm as bald as most of my teachers. But I'm still readily frightened. And I still feel like a child.

And the few schoolfriends I've kept in touch with still seem like children to me. Some sag, some bristle, all are battered, but they are still recognisable as the vulnerable, fear-prone, error-prone children they were.

Is all adulthood a sham, a theatrical role, a performance to daunt the tinies? Was Hammersley as vulnerable as I am? I suppose he was. But still it doesn't seem so. Still it seems that when my generation came of age the world of men shrank. A tribe of heroes and ogres passed from the earth and left behind a race of scuttling pygmies. It seemed so apt that the boy who became head prefect in my final year, the boy who tried to play the role that Hammersley had played, to fill the ten-league boots that Hammersley had worn, went by the name of Weatherseed. We knew him as Budgie.

Weltschmerzcroc

Generally the English language will do to express one's disappointment in the human animal. Cor blimey, you can say, everybody's nuts. And if you say it loudly enough and often enough and smack a few inanimate objects around, then it's just about okay. It relieves the stress, gives you the sort of feeling you get on emptying a distended bladder, and you are able to return with a degree of equanimity to blameless solitary afternoons of Lego and peanut butter sandwiches.

But there are moments when the English language, for all its flexibility and breadth, just isn't up to the job, and you find yourself obliged to reach, oh dear, for a hunk of German. I don't speak German. I can and do say 'leather trousers' with the fluency of a native, but after that zilch. Except, that is, for the stuff of gloom. The Germans, for understandable reasons, are world-leaders at gloom.

So when it all gets too much, I just lower a bucket into the well of compound nouns and throat-tearing consonants that is the German language and draw up a bit of guttural misery. And the best bit, the bit I've got between my teeth right now, 6.30 on a Tuesday morning with nor-west clouds overarching and threatening another day of insupportable heat and armpits like Sumatra, is weltschmerz. It means literally world-pain, but it sounds so right you don't need to know that. There are times when weltschmerz is inescapable and one such time is now. Because of croc-man.

Don't pretend you don't know who I mean by croc-man. He's the chubby Aussie who looks like Shane Warne without the urbane sophistication. He makes televisual pornography about animals. He exudes a transparently bogus zest that makes him shout when he's whispering, and he wears worrying scoutmaster clothes and he specialises in irritating crocodiles and he does it all with a feel-good conservationist theme to conceal the truth that it's mere titillation for the timid urban masses. I don't know if the Germans have knocked up a word for this sort of television. If not, I would like to propose dumkrapschmalz.

Well, it seems that croc-man also does his stunts in a cage for the edification of fat tourists. And so as to make it even more edifying he lugs his six-minute-old son into the cage to baptise him in the profitable art of humiliating reptiles. He claims that he's teaching the child to be, in his own honeyed words, croc savvy. Why the cross-eyed infant needs to be croc savvy I have no idea, since even if it does learn to recognise that the saurian in front of it is both peckish and approaching at speed, that's of no use to a blob too young to crawl away.

But anyway, there's croc-man, kiddiwink under one arm, croc at his feet, microphone at his mouth and audience on the other side of some stout wire. I've seen the photo in the paper. The audience, oh my God, look at them. Fat, bored, brain-dead, and augmenting their eyes and memory with camcorders bought from Harvey Norman in the Boxing Day sales. I don't know what they do for you, but for me they bring great gouts of weltschmerz rumbling over the horizon like a squadron of Messerschmitts.

But that's barely the start of it. What's really got the weltschmerz buzzing is the uproar about the baby. One slip of the foot, screams the Society for Finding Something to Moan About, and that child is croc-lunch. Yes, yes, of course, of course, just as any baby sitting on Daddy's shoulders is one slip of Daddy's foot away from landing head-first on the pavement. Whether a croc toddles along to clean up the mess will be irrelevant. And just as any child strapped into a horrible Japanese sedan is one parental sneeze away from a head-on encounter with a lamppost, and just as . . . oh, forget it. The world is a risky place. You look after your kids and let ghastly croc-man look after his.

But the child, they scream, is being exploited. Yes of course it's being exploited. So is your child when you ditch it in front of advertisements for My Hideous Little Pony or Let'sPlayMurderStation. If you want to go and stop a bit of exploitation go fly to San Salvador and save the hundred thousand kids picking a toxic living from the smoking trash heaps of the rich. Or those lovely bits of Asia where the twelve-year-olds have got that far in life on six grains of rice a day and where the lucky ones with dextrous fingers weave carpets to gratify the greed of us fatsos in the west, and the unlucky ones are sold into sexual slavery for other not so very different fatsos.

You probably won't do any good, but you might stop pointing a pointless finger, transferring your guilt, having no sense of propor-tion, bellowing your own unacknowledged fear, and giving me weltschmerz.

Between us and dust

Otorohanga (pronounced 'North Island town of no account') has become a town of some account. It has appointed itself the capital of Kiwiana. The locals have bedecked their humdrum main street with giant versions of the things that make this country this country. It is a parade of predictabilities. There are sheep and kiwifruit and pavlovas and jandals and sheep. But apparently the tourists – that vast tribe of the bored who long for their holidays to end so they can go home and tell the neighbours how much they didn't want their holidays to end – flock.

In Otorohanga the English tourists can gawp at their own sheep, the Australians at their own dessert, the Chinese at their own gooseberries and the Japanese at their own footwear. For the jandal, that local institution, is as Kiwi as ju-jitsu.

In Great Britain the jandal's a flip-flop, in North America it's a thong, but in Japan it's simply what they've been shuffling around in since they first pushed rice into mud.

The very word jandal admits as much. It's a contraction of Japanese sandal. For confirmation I looked it up in the *Oxford English*

Dictionary – not, I should point out, the *Shorter OED*, nor yet my old pal the *Concise OED*, but rather the granddaddy *OED*, the big one, the compendious everything of the most widespread language in the world, the twenty-volume took-a-century-to-compile *OED*. And there between Jan (January, abbrev.) and Janders (jaundice, colloq. obs.) I found, well, nothing. The *OED* doesn't recognise the jandal. But you do and I do, and so does the rest of the world.

For the jandal is a global thing. It is the world's cheapest footwear. From the steaming trash heaps of Sao Paolo to the teeming brothels of Bangkok, the jandal puts half an inch of foam rubber between the dominant animal species and the dust he sprang from.

And in the forty or so years since the leather sandal of Japan turned into the universal sandal of summer, it has evolved. Today the shelves of the Warehouse offer jandals with inch-thick soles, with contoured soles, with soles of little nipples. There are flowered jandals, velcro jandals, see-through jandals, jelly jandals. And none of these are jandals. They are too fancy. The true jandal is as minimalist as Japanese gardening.

It is a sole and a strap. The sole has an off-white veneer. The underside is anaemic blue or anaemic red. So is the strap. That strap is stamped with a crude motif and is held in place by three little plugs. And that's it. The lot. The jandal.

It's the shoe you're wearing when you're not wearing a shoe. It cannot be worn with socks except by holidaying bureaucrats and a toothless man I sometimes fish with. The jandal will carry you across blistering sands and melting asphalt. It is amphibious. It floats. It can be shed in an instant. It makes a serviceable door-wedge, an outstanding fly-swat and a fine noise against a fat thigh.

Running in jandals is a perilous art. Gripping the sweaty sole requires the toes of a gibbon. Few of us have the toes of a gibbon. Sooner or later the tip of the sole of a running jandal catches on the ground and curls back on itself and your impetus pulls the plug through the sole.

When you sit up and dust yourself down you find a flap of skin hanging from your big toe and the remains of your jandal hanging from your ankle. And that's that. The jandal is finished. Once the plug has pulled through, it will pull through again. You can push it back in, but for ever afterwards you will be walking on treachery. It is time to toss the jandal, walk barefoot to the beachfront store and part with another $1.95. But that's easier to write than to do.

For an old jandal is like a familiar lover. One side of the sole is still as fat as a steak, but the other has worn as thin as a slice of ham. The things slopes as you slope. At the heels and the toes the white veneer has disappeared so it looks like a footprint in blue sand. The straps have moulded to a bulge in the shape of a heart, a heart that fits your foot and yours alone. To toss this out is an amputation. And what you're amputating is the best of your past. For you wore that jandal when the weather was warm and you were free and things were simple. Trashing a jandal is like burying a songbird of summer. Even in Otorohanga.

Night-time angels

Do you have night-time angels? I do. Mine are good at crosswords.

I like a cryptic crossword but often there will be one clue that baffles me. I'll pursue a line of thinking that appears to be the right one but that brings me up against a wall of wrongness. So I will leave the clue alone a while and think of other things, then readdress it. But when I readdress it I will find my head pursuing the selfsame route for a second time, then a third time, a whole series of times, until it is sore from butting the unshiftable and I'll retire to bed bleeding with defeat and jeered every step of the way by the incomplete grid.

Then in the night the angels come. They take the chance to work when my stubbornness is sleeping. And in the morning as I shuffle to the source of coffee and fill a cup and idly spot the crossword, up pops the answer as fresh and surprising and clean as a morning mushroom. It's all the angels' work.

But they're not so good at careers. Last night a woman asked me what I'd like to be if I had all of human history to choose from. I could be pharaoh or pharisee, fisherman or fakir, anything I liked. I said I didn't know.

The night-time angels did. And now, on this dark winter morning when the cat is more than usually keen to leap onto the desk and type with its paws, the angels have pronounced. If I had all the choices in the history of human life I'd like to be a wandering minstrel. A troubadour.

I'd own nothing but a lute, a dog, a horse, a hat and a headful of songs. Illiterate, lice-racked. I would travel from pre-medieval village to pre-medieval village, climbing on arrival to some point of prominence, a balcony above the village square perhaps, or, on my naughtier days, a loaded gibbet. I'd strum a chord or two as an aesthetic bait to lure the stinking peasants, and then I'd sing the news. And what news. None of the pettiness of the mundane, but grand and sweeping news, made memorable by rhyme and tune and art. I'd sing of kings whose bodies rotted underneath their finery, of some ancient lover cutting off a finger and sending it by bird of paradise to her he loved. I'd sing of wars and famines, avalanches and the luminous ghosts of fish.

The peasants down below would gawp and coo and cackle as appropriate and toss me buns and pennies and would stroke my dog. On good days they would give me flagons full of ale and for the night a truckle bed of hay.

On bad days I would have to mount my horse and gallop out of town, my head held low behind the horse's neck to miss the hail of ribaldry and flung things. I'd seek a hedge to sleep beneath, all wet and shivering and wrapped around my dog.

Yes, that would be the life, a life of rapid ups and downs and rootlessness, with no diurnal work, but only risk and fear and sudden headspin joy.

But the angels are impractical. For starters I am terrified of horses. No herbivores have need of teeth as big as those. For another thing I am not brave. And for a third and final thing, I know I cannot sing.

I'd love to sing. I try to constantly. With beer inside me I can't resist the karaoke mike. But I murder every song.

I once took singing lessons. I yearned to play a luscious part in *Cabaret*, the part played in the film by Joel Gray, the part of the MC. So slinky, zestful, packed with acid, comic, perspicacious and a sexual omnivore – in short a catalogue of greatness.

I went to a woman who sings like a bubbling spring and I said teach me, and I flung dollars at her for a series of five lessons. But I attended only three. When I sang what she sang I could hear my notes were wrong but I was powerless to right them. She said the nicest things but she was lying. I ran at tunes just as I ran at crossword clues until my forehead bled from butting against the unshiftable bricks of inability.

I think I hoped that if I persevered the angels of the night might come and sweetly readjust the faulty tuning forks that occupy my head. I hoped in vain. The angels never came. They never will.

Why it is that we should yearn for what we cannot do and at the same time undervalue what we can, I cannot tell you. All I know is that if I could I would sing you a song. 'No wandering minstrel I,' I'd sing, 'no thing of rags and patches.' But I think I'll just start a crossword. The angels can finish it.

Talking lousy

Lousy Language is booming. According to the Society for Lousy Language, which administers the sport and has recently incorporated the Cliché Club, which was stony broke, and snapped up the Inappropriate Simile Society like a rat up a drainpipe, anyone can play. A spokesman for the Dead Metaphor branch of the society said that they welcomed new players with open arms.

And it is with the variant of the game called Dead Metaphors that most beginners start. The key skill a beginner has to master in order to play is to learn to use metaphors like key skill without thought to their meaning. After that he needs only a handful of exhausted similes and he's in like Flynn.

Some players are content to spend their lives at this level, but those with a natural propensity for Lousy Language soon realise that dead metaphors are two a penny. So they specialise. A popular early specialisation that many people like at the beginning is Redundancy and Repetition. It can be played over and above the basic fundamental game of Lousy Language and has proved so popular that there's now a great big club entirely devoted to it.

But even Repetition and Redundancy can pall and grow dull, and rather than lingering within its limited confines most serious Lousy Language enthusiasts head off in search of Milton's fresh fields and pastures new. A few fetch up briefly in Novelty Coinages, a small and specialised competition dominated for the last three years by a single player. His threepeat of successes understandably daunts newcomers who are afraid of becoming perpetual cellar dwellers in the Novelty Coinage league. And when they further realise that today's novelty coinage is tomorrow's dead metaphor they often choose not to put in the hard yards.

They have plenty of other options. A few find pleasure in the Euphemisms competition although the disadvantaged and under-privileged sometimes find it challenging. A more popular choice is Mixed Metaphors. Here many Lousy Linguists find that they can really branch out and spread their wings. Indeed some of them are hooked on mixed metaphors just as soon as they dip their toe in the water. And once hooked they're up and running. The danger that the Mixed Metaphor player must always beware is thought. If for one moment he pauses to reflect on the meaning of his metaphors his game will collapse. Any suspicion of thought must be nipped immediately and ruthlessly in the bud before being kicked firmly into touch. Otherwise the player will find that he's cooked his goose by shooting himself in the foot.

He can even find himself shifting accidentally into the highly specialised field of Unintentionally Saying the Opposite of What You Mean. Numbers in this game are literally exploding. It is impossible to underestimate its popularity.

The Society for Lousy Language is keen to stress that Lousy Language is more than just a game. Proficiency in any one of its thousand variations can significantly enhance employment prospects, most obviously in journalism and broadcasting. Many amateur Lousy

Linguists have gone on to become highly paid sports commentators. But Lousy Language opens doors to many less expected fields. The civil service, for example, is crammed with Lousy Linguists. According to the society spokesman, Wellington boasts more players of a Lousy Language variant called Obscurantist Stuffing than any socioeconomically comparable urban environment in the country. And many of them are in positions that afford substantive remuneration. They have to hire a porter to lug home their fiscal envelopes.

The Lousy Linguist also has the world of commerce at his feet. Once he has learned to monitor strategic developments going forward, or at least in the medium term, then the sky's the limit. In other words, said the spokesman, Lousy Language games are the ideal training ground for the managers of tomorrow, and he cited the example of Mr Christopher 'Chris' Moller as a model for all aspiring Lousy Linguists.

'Here is a man,' said the spokesman, 'who has had a glittering career in industry and has now risen to be head of the Rugby Football Union and SANZAR. But he has never forgotten his debt to Lousy Language. Here, for example, is the reply he gave only last week to a question about television revenue. "To suggest that a drop in one market is going to translate to a 50 per cent drop in the total global revenue for SANZAR is a very long bow to draw."

'Forget the redundancy of "total global",' said the spokesman, wiping joyous moisture from the corner of one eye, 'forget the misuse of translate, and concentrate on the bow metaphor. There you see a master at work. Could anyone beat that image for sheer impenetrability? It goes beyond cliché. It climbs to dazzling heights of meaninglessness. I gawp at its genius. It represents everything that we at the society stand for. But was Mr Moller satisfied? No he wasn't. He went further. With a skill that leaves me speechless he improved on the unimprovable. "It was a very wide miss of the goalposts," he said. Beat that.'

Hello, heat

Heat's back. Hello, heat. Laden with steam and indolence it swung down yesterday from the waistband of the globe, dumped its wet on the Alps then came to my house. It came like an oven-door opening.

I drew the blinds. The heat laid siege, slowly. It seeped through the cracks and went everywhere and stayed. It occupied the middle and the corners. It filled the space under my desk, made my feet slide on my jandals. It turned the dog's water bowl on the deck to the temperature of blood. It killed insects and sprinkled the water with the corpses. They floated like tiny screws of paper, wispy, spent, burnt.

My dog has a black fur coat. In the heat she was like Trotsky in Mexico. Unlike Trotsky she couldn't shed her coat. The air heated her up, flopped her down, opened her jaws and tweaked out her tongue. The heat drove her under the house and pushed her over onto her side, panting.

Down below in the port it made windscreens into fireflashes. It made vinyl car seats screamingly untouchable. It made supermarket bags pudgy.

I am a cool climate man. I don't mind warmth. But warmth isn't heat. Warmth is a kindness. Warmth says do. Heat says don't.

Hot countries are poor countries. Samoa is poor. El Salvador's poor. Sudan is very poor. In hot countries they put on long white cotton shirts and sit down. They sit in the shade with a hat and a beer and patience. Sit it out. Try not to bother. Sit it out. Heat bleaches and saps. Bleaches the land, saps the will.

At twenty-one I went teaching in Spain and met heat for the first time. It was heat like brass. I didn't know what to do. I didn't know to do nothing. I flitted from shade patch to shade patch. I taught in the Spanish summer as I would in a Danish winter. I taught till the sweat darkened the crotch of my trousers, till my my neck boiled with boils.

The fan in my classroom broke down one morning. I was teaching six middle-aged women. They conferred, then took pity. They took me away to an underground bar and fed me beer and a cold omelette. They taught me fretlessness. It doesn't matter, said the women. Today it is hot. That is all it is.

The only hot countries that are rich are the countries with oil. They were poor countries for ever, but then the busy greedy pale men came from the cool places with equipment made of metal that grew too hot to be handled. The pale men drilled through the rock and laid pipelines, sucking the liquefied heat of the desert away to put feeling in the fingers of the north. The locals took the money and sat in the shade of their thick white walls to drink sweet tea and watch the pale men being busy.

Last year I went to Singapore. The heat there was wet. The air wouldn't take my sweat. It was too full. It was always an inch away from rain, sudden, brief and rampant rain that was warm and that drenched and then stopped. After it had stopped the island steamed. I hated all of it.

Yesterday I had to work. I worked badly, listless with heat. The keyboard was sticky. My head was torpid. Invention wilted. There was grit in the vees between my fingers. The desk fan skimmed ash from the ashtray. I gave up and drove the dog to the bay. The road ahead of us danced with black heat.

My dog ran into the water to shoulder depth then just stood there, reviving. One minute in water took a decade off her age. Cool again, she bounded through the wavelets like a spring-loaded puppy, like a lithe black dolphin.

Two women lay on their backs on towels, like starfish in bikinis, surrendering as if dead. Few men do that. I think some women are reptiles.

I swam with my dog. She snorts as she swims. I like to swim on my side to watch her legs working under water. Dogs don't really swim. Naturally buoyant, they just float and run. My old dog can swim for miles.

The soil of the path behind the bay was dried to talcum powder. The leaves of the sheltering trees, still pale green and spring tender, diffused the sunlight to something gentle. But you could sense the effect of the sun on them. You could sense them darkening, thickening, ageing. Two months from now they'll be leathery. Four months and they'll crackle underfoot.

Back home and the house was a vat of heat. I fed myself, fed my dog, then stripped and lay on my bed, sweating, riding it out.

Little Ms Coke

According to a report in the newspaper last week, researchers at the British National Archives have discovered a girl born in Yorkshire in 1379. Most medieval girls had names like Godolena or Helwise, but not this little girl. She was called Diot Coke. I am not making this up. Diot is a diminutive form of Dionisia, and Coke is a variant form of Cook. Variant form is a philologist's term for spelling mistake.

Interest in the discovery has been so intense that a production company has turned the life of the Coke family into a soap opera for television. I am making this up.

Episode 1. The setting: a hovel in medieval Yorkshire. Mrs Coke is at the sink peeling a goat. Little Diot erupts into the room, flings her school bokes across the floor and bursts into tears.

Mrs Coke: Oh, my little Diot. Come to Mummy. Let me enfold you in my comforting medieval bosom that smells of honey and goat-flesh and tooth decay. We may not live long in the fourteenth century but we do live close to…

Diot: Boo hoo.

Mrs Coke: Shh dear, I'm setting the scene. As I was saying, we fourteenth-century peasants may live brief and simple lives blighted by poverty and goat shortages and gingivitis, but we do live close to nature. Many years from now, people in dreadful cable-knit sweaters will sing folk songs about how happy our hard lives were. Now, where were we? Ah yes, what's the matter with my little Diot?

Diot: Oh Mother, why do you always talk about the future?

Mrs Coke: Because, my darling, I've got powers that other folk don't have. I can see down the long meadow of time into the goat paddock of tomorrow. That's why we called you Diot Coke.

Diot (exploding into tears again like a bottle of fizzy drink left out in the sun): Oh, why couldn't I have an ordinary name like Godolena or Helwise?

Mrs Coke: There there, my darling. Have those nasty boys at school been making fun of your name again? Have they, my little Diot?

Diot snuffles and nods and sinks deeper into the maternal bosom.

Mrs Coke: Dry your eyes, my little one. Your time will come. Six hundred and twenty-five years from now Diot Coke won't just be the baked apple of my eye. She'll be world famous. She'll be a brand name.

Diot: Tell me what a brand name is again, Mother.

Mrs Coke: Well, my darling, a brand name is something you can't see or touch or eat. It's just a name that people believe in.

Diot: You mean like God?

Mrs Coke: Well, sort of, yes. And when people believe in something it becomes very valuable. One day, my darling, your name will be worth millions of groats.

Diot: Don't you mean goats, Mother?

Mrs Coke: Of course I do. Silly me. Anyway, one day your name will be worth more goats than you can count, more goats than even the squire's got. Because when people believe in something, they're happy to exchange their goats for it. They'll hand over those goats for a brand name faster than you can say gullibility.

Diot: Tomorrow's people sound terribly silly, Mother.

Mrs Coke: Well, dear, they'll have been subject to an awful lot of advertising. That's what we call lying. But don't you worry your pretty little head about that. I don't pretend to understand it all myself. But I do know that the time will come when you will thank me for ... are you listening to me?

She isn't. Diot's head has plunged so deeply into the maternal breast that it's invisible.

Mrs Coke: What is it now, my little Diot? Don't you want to be a brand name?

With a rich slurping noise, Diot extracts her darling face and raises it towards her mother. Tears of pure saccharine cascade down her cheeks to the earthen floor where they're sucked up noisily by the family pig.

Diot: But Mother, why do I have to be so skinny? Nasty Jack Dothegoat, the squire's son, said I looked like a darning needle and all the boys laughed. Oh why can't I be plump like my sisters?

Mrs Coke: O Diot, how many times do I have to explain to you? Your sisters are different. Both Regula and Vanilla are crammed with sugar. That's why they're such a nice shape. But you, my little artificial sweetness, are the shape of tomorrow. You may find this hard to believe, but 625 years from now when there's plenty of goats for everyone to eat, all the girls will want to look as if they haven't seen a goat steak in months. They'll want to look like starvelings, like boys. And that's when my little Diot Coke will come into her own. They'll call you the real thing.

Diot: What does that mean?

Mrs Coke: Nothing at all, but that doesn't matter. You've got a wonderful future, my darling. Tomorrow is yours.

Episode ends with mother and daughter standing together watching the sun rise to a backing track of advertising theme tunes.

Next week: A medieval boy recently discovered by Swedish archivists comes to Diot's school. His name is Svenn Oop. Svenn and Diot fall madly in love and want to merge behind the bike sheds. But the Medieval Monopolies Commission, headed by evil Squire Dothegoat, stands between them and perpetual carbonated happiness.

Probe and rectify, please

When Prue from the Therapeutic Massage Association rang to ask if I would like a therapeutic massage, I thought that I wouldn't. But I also thought of baboons.

I've always envied baboons. Not for the purple buttocks, though there are occasions when a couple of those could prove handy, or at least entertaining, but for the way baboons groom each other. They pass hot African afternoons poring over each other's flesh, running their prehensile fingers through the fur, extracting ticks and eating them.

I'm not frantic to eat ticks but I would like to be at ease with touch. Touch is potent. If I am working at my desk and someone unexpectedly lays hands on my shoulders, a spasm of distaste makes my muscles cringe and tense. And I can still remember from adolescence a hand placed casually on my forearm that stood the hairs on my neck to attention and triggered a month of lovesick sleeplessness.

So when Prue offered me a therapeutic massage, I dithered.

'But,' said Prue, 'you'll enjoy it and it will make you feel good and it will cost you nothing.' So I said yes.

Frances operates from what looks like a garage. She has a diploma in therapeutic massage. Whether this makes her a masseur or a masseuse or just someone with a diploma in therapeutic massage, I didn't ask. I just called her Frances. She was infectiously cheerful.

The garage had anatomical posters on the wall, carpet on the floor and a table on the carpet. The air was warm and awash with subliminal new-age musak that I didn't like but soon stopped noticing.

I completed a have-you-ever-suffered-from-any-of-these form that made me wonder how I'd survived so long, wrote no for everything, stripped to my underpants and lay on my front on the table. Frances draped me with towels. My face rested in a padded basketball hoop.

Then Frances warmed her hands, smeared them with almond oil, shifted a towel in the manner of a morgue attendant seeking identification and set to work on a leg. Her thumbs ploughed through my muscles like the prow of a ship through a sea of soft rubber.

When I asked her why she used almond oil she said it was just personal taste. 'Some people use apricot oil,' she said, 'or grapeseed oil.'

I said I used grapeseed oil to fry sausages.

'So do I,' she said.

In my right calf she found what I sensed to be a medium density lump. When she pressed it, it felt a bit sore.

'That feels a bit sore,' I said.

'I know,' she said.

Then she asked me whether I wanted a superficial feel-good massage or a deep one that would probe and rectify the sore and lumpy bits.

'Probe and rectify,' I said.

'You'll feel it in the morning,' she said and her thumbs plunged. It felt as though she were parting sheaves of muscle fibre in order to get at the undersheaves. She returned to the knotted lumpy bit and leant on it till it burned with a low-intensity doing-me-good pain. Gradually the lump dissolved, as if melting under heat and pressure.

When she'd finished with the leg she asked if it felt lighter. By now I was as keen as a dog to please. I waved the leg around a bit.

'I don't know,' I said.

After she'd rooted around on the other leg for a minute or two I told her that she had found a sore spot somewhere but that I wasn't going to tell her where it was.

'Let's see if my thumbs return to it,' she said, which sounded altogether too mystical for me. Her thumbs returned to it.

She compressed my buttocks agreeably for a bit then moved up my back. When she reached the shoulder I told her of an ancient injury that still niggles. She replied with an anatomical analysis that sounded reassuringly medical and followed it up with some lovely lump-melting stuff in the area that Mr Spock uses to kill people.

I rolled over and she did the front of my legs and then asked if I'd like my stomach done. I said yes. She told me she'd attended a three-day course on stomach massage. When I asked what there was in stomach muscles to occupy three days, she explained how it was possible to rummage under the muscles to get at the internal organs. Shortly afterwards she told me my stomach was very tense.

When she'd done with me she asked how long I thought I'd been on the table. I said about an hour. It had been almost two.

'So how do you feel?' she asked.

I said I wasn't sure and I thanked her and I left.

A little way along the road I stopped my car and went walkabout. I wanted to feel how I felt. I felt loose. I felt light on my feet. And I felt about half an inch taller.

I slept like a baby, one of those babies that smell faintly of almonds. In the morning I felt dandy. I took the dogs up the hill as I do every day. I loped up that hill like a baboon.

The girls done good

Girl. It's a good word, solid, consonantal, plainly Anglo-Saxon in origin, like swine and kick and sprat. I heard it used on National Radio recently. Geoff Robinson used it when crossing to an expert who was going to tell us about a Kiwi victory in pool play in the Netball World Cup. 'Another good win for the girls,' said Mr Robinson.

I've never met Mr Robinson but I admire him. He rarely if ever goes aggressively for an interviewee but he sees through cant with splendid clarity and poses the mean question with a half-laugh and a lightness of tone that disguises the knife in the ribs. I like that.

Anyway he crossed to the netball expert who was as dreary of voice as most netball experts seem to be. Netball saddens me a bit. It seems so restrictive a game. The New Zealanders, now crowned as the best team in the world, are spectacular athletes. They run like prairie dogs, change direction faster than the birds of the air, leap like salmon and still manage to smile. But they aren't allowed to leave their ascribed areas on the court. Irene will only ever stand at one end. Never once in her career will she have the chance to chat with the magnificently vivacious Vilimaina with the pogo stick legs and the refusal to take care of her body. The two are separated by 25 metres of pedantry. Every major game's a whistle-fest. I wish they had a sport that gave full rein to their athletic talents.

So, Ms Dreary delivered her report and those of us who were still awake heard Mr Robinson return to air and apologise. 'Sorry,' he said, 'I shouldn't have said girls. I should have said women.' And if your windows rattled around 8.30am on the morning of Friday the 18th of July and the cat dived under the sofa and your baby started to cry, well it's my turn to apologise. I have large lungs.

Fast forward to the moments after the final. Joy abounded. The superbly partisan Jamaican crowd was doing impromptu revelry and the television interviewer had secured the Kiwi coach, the wonderful Ruth Aitken. Wonderful because she is charming, gracious, cheerful, articulate, cool under pressure and transparently warm of heart. She flings into the shade the coaches of every other sporting team in this country, except the Warriors coach, the Aussie whose name I forget, whose every word has the twinkle of honesty to it and who never forgets that it's just a game.

'I'm unbelievably proud of the girls,' said Ms Aitken. Five of those six words may not be verbatim. But one of them is, and that word is 'girls'. I know so. I paid very close attention.

Cut again to an interview with the unstoppably grinning Anna Rowberry. 'I'm unbelievably proud of the girls,' said Ms Rowberry. Five of those six words may not be verbatim. But one of them is, and that word is 'girls'. I know so. I paid very close attention.

So why can't Mr Robinson call them girls? Because, the strident ones will say, 'girls' is demeaning. Many of these women are married with children. Mothers are not girls.

Well, for a start, these mothers seem happy enough to call them-selves girls which seems pretty solid evidence to me that they don't find it demeaning. And if we step across the sexual abyss for a second and consider the All Blacks, many of them are married with children too. But 'The boys played good', is their unfailing post-match refrain or, in recent weeks, 'real good'.

Perhaps so, say the strident ones who have infiltrated Mr Robinson's and my own head and made us tread through the field of sexual politics as if it were mined, it's different for the blokes. The words boy and girl have different connotations. One approves, the other belittles.

Oh no it doesn't. Even a four-year-old Peruvian learning English at el kindergarten can tell you that boy and girl are precisely parallel terms, like aunt and uncle, brother and sister, mother and father.

Furthermore, in the context of sport they are appropriate, because sport is what young things do. Using boys and girls to describe sports players acknowledges that however hard they work at it, it is only, in the end, a game, a childish game, and it doesn't matter all that much.

And that usage is implicitly understood by all who speak the language. A group of pensioner women who splendidly get together to do formation marching or to play bowls will always refer to their mob as 'the girls'. That's not indoctrination. That's not subordination. That's acknowledgement only that what they're doing is unserious. They may be eighty but they are playing the games of children. Like netballers. Like rugby players. Like boys. Like girls.

And if you're still not convinced that Mr Robinson was right to use the word, and if you're about to pick up a pen and write me a letter in cyanide, well go ahead. I am still boy enough to enjoy a chuckle. And man enough, I hope, to feel sad, too.

Crapeau dans le trou

There are daily miracles – waking up, the silk of a dog's ears, coffee – and then there are annual miracles – like sex, spring and toad in the hole.

Toad in the hole is an evocative name for a foodstuff. It evokes, well, holes with toads in them. But it evokes even more in French. Crapeau dans le trou evokes a mop and a lot of disinfectant.

But I have never heard of crapeau dans le trou, presumably because toad in the hole is Anglo-Saxon cuisine. To a Frenchman Anglo-Saxon cuisine is an oxymoron.

Toad in the hole involves batter and chipolatas. If the French made it, it would involve herbs, a complicated sauce and toads.

I'm glad the French don't make it. I like toads. They are not the slimy creatures that people imagine, and they jump. They don't jump with especial vigour – it's more of a languid lollop – but any sort of jump is a pleasing thing in a beast. Riffling through my mental encyclopaedia of natural history I find that I warm to grasshoppers, frogs, kangaroos, to everything, indeed, that jumps, except for fleas. And horses.

It isn't the jumping that I dislike in horses. It's the horses themselves. I am frightened of them. They have back legs. They have mobile bristling nostrils. And they have teeth the size of shoe-horns. I find those teeth suspicious. They seem much larger than Dobbin needs merely to eat grass. And anyway I'm not convinced that Dobbin could grow to be a full-sized Dobbin on grass alone. The evidence suggests that horses are carnivores. Presumably nocturnal ones.

They hunt at night so that we suspect nothing and little girls continue to go sentimentally gaga over them. They use those bristling rubbery nostrils (the horses, that is, and not the gullible girls, whose nostrils are still forty years short of bristling) to sniff out bits of meat such as stoats, rabbits or toads that are unwise enough to have left their holes. Having sniffed flesh, the horses turn round and sneak up on their prey in reverse until they are close enough to unleash those back legs and boot their victims suddenly into oblivion and the next paddock. They then jump over the fence, dine at leisure by the light of the moon, run their monstrous tongues round their prehensile lips in order to remove all traces of blood, jump back over the fence and are standing there placidly at dawn looking all my-little-pony with eyelashes when Miss Sentiment arrives with her saddle and her lump of sugar.

The French may not have cottoned onto toad in the hole but they've rumbled the horses. They eat them. When I lived in France I did too.

I also once ate frog. It tasted of chicken. Or, to be precise, it tasted of very little chicken. The dish is advertised as frogs' legs but actually it's only the thighs. What the French do with the shins I can't tell you. Maybe they toss them to the horses.

But I never ate toads, and nor do the French, which is something of a miracle. But it's not the annual miracle of toad in the hole.

The miracle doesn't lie in the chipolatas. It lies in the batter. To make the batter you require a little volcano of flour. Into the caldera go two eggs and a dash of milk. You swirl the dash and the eggs around a bit, creating little lava flows over the lip, which is all good fun in a practical geography sort of way, then you gradually dissolve the volcano itself, adding more milk as you go and beating all the while like Mr Squeers the schoolmaster.

According to the recipe book the stuff should achieve the consistency of cream. Mine achieved the consistency of cream with lumps in it, but I solved the problem of the lumps by ignoring them.

Having beaten my batter, all I had to do was fry the chipolatas, and heat a baking tray to such glowing incandescence that I could, had I so wished, have beaten it into horseshoes. Then I dropped a bit of butter in, enjoyed the bubbling and smoking and noise for a bit, and tipped in the batter and the sausages.

I pulled up a chair to the oven door. There is a glass panel in that door through which it is possible to observe nothing at all because of seven years of accumulated impenetrabilia. But after ten minutes, I opened the oven door a crack, let the blast of heat peel the skin from my face and beheld the miracle. The cream with lumps had stopped being cream with lumps. It had fluffed and risen. It had become a golden cloud. Why, I've no idea. How, I've no idea. It was like the miracle of creation. I pulled the tray from the oven and carved off about an acre of cloud. I was salivating like Niagara.

So why is this miracle merely annual? Because it takes a year to forget how bad it is. Toad in the hole is pap. It's nursery food. The chipolatas taste of nothing and the cloud of less. The dog got most of it. It tastes like crapeau dans le trou. The French are wise.

Dogtape

081/22561361 is not a promising name for a dog.

A dog's name needs to be simple and unremarkable, because there will be times when you need to summon the dog from embarrassing situations such as a picnic on the beach. There is a lot to be said for a dog eating a picnic on the beach, but rather less to be said for it when the picnic is someone else's. So you need a name that attracts the dog's attention but does not attract attention to the dog. In such circumstances a name like 'Ferlinghetti' is unhelpful. So is 'Fire'. And 081/22561361 is not a lot better.

But that is how I first knew this dog. The dog was a gift. A friend acquired the dog for me in Australia without asking, and posted it over. I got a telephone call from a nice man in Auckland telling me how to collect 081/22561361 from Christchurch airport. He said that the paperwork might take a while so I would be wise to do it on the day before 081/22561361 flew into Christchurch. The man was right.

When I described the dog as a gift I was using the word in a technical sense. Gift in this sense means something that costs the receiver a lot of money. For the cash that I laid out at Christchurch airport I could have bought just over 100 Dalmatians and taken them all to the cinema. Twice. With lollies at half-time. (Assuming that there is still half-time and that there are still lollies available. I no longer go to the cinema because I can't smoke, take a dog or understand why I have paid money to listen to people eating in the dark.)

At the cargo depot a nice man filled out an abundance of forms and then gave me a map of the airport. I had to go next to customs which he marked with an X, and then to MAF which he marked with an X, and then back to the cargo depot which he marked with an X even though I'd already found it.

Call me cantankerous but I asked why I had to return to the cargo depot. Because, said the man, he had to sell me a little sticker to affix to the MAF clearance papers and he didn't want me to lose it. I asked why he couldn't give me the sticker now and then I could stick it on the MAF forms myself. He said the sticker cost $22 and he didn't want me to lose it. I said I was willing to take the risk and paid him $22.

There was another nice man in customs with wrapover hair and a shirt under pressure. The stretches between the shirt buttons gaped like vertical eyes. He told me that I had to pay GST on the value of the dog. I said the dog was a gift in the traditional sense and that the man in Auckland had told me that, because I didn't plan to breed from the dog or to sell it but merely to eat other people's beach picnics with it, I wouldn't have to pay GST on it. Mr Wrapover told me with a highly amused snort that distorted the eyes on his shirt, that they didn't know much in Auckland. I paid GST on the dog.

Or rather I paid GST on the market value of the dog. I use the term 'market value' in the technical sense, which means a sum arrived at by taking the number of staplers on the customs desk and multiplying by the square of the date.

And then Mr Wrapover, towards whom I was feeling increasingly warm, told me I had to pay GST on the freight.

'I'm sorry?' I said, though I wasn't. I was uncomprehending. But Mr Wrapover explained.

'You've got to pay GST on the freight,' he said.

'Oh,' I said, 'I understand now. I have to pay a tax levied on New Zealand goods and services on a sum of money already paid in Australian dollars, in Australia, by an Australian, to an Australian airline, a sum, furthermore, on which the Australian government has already levied its own GST.'

'You've got it,' said Mr Wrapover, evidently pleased with his explanatory prowess.

Call me cantankerous but I said that I thought this was theft.

'Do you want the dog?' said Mr Wrapover. Levering myself off the barrel over which I found myself, I paid GST on the freight.

After customs, MAF was frankly a disappointment. Their requirements cost me five minutes, no arguments and a mere $28. And they gave me a piece of paper on which to stick my $22 sticker which, remarkably, I hadn't lost.

So now all that was left for me to do was to hire a wheelbarrow to ferry the documentation home, go to bed, fail to sleep for the excitement, return to the airport the next day, show them the wheelbarrow, go round the back, find a crate wrapped in red tape, take the shears to the tape and open the door.

Scattering tape as he came and exuding gales of ununiformed, unofficial, un-carbon-copy-in-triplicate exuberance, 081/22561361 leapt out of the crate and into my heart.

SQAC

In the same week that the Alcoholic Liquor Advisory Council published its survey of the nation's drinking habits and revealed that more than half the population is going to pop its cork at an early age because of its enthusiasm for popping corks, the Survey and Questionnaire Advisory Council has published a survey on New Zealand's consumption of surveys.

'The survey,' said a SQAC spokesman, 'confirms what we suspected: New Zealand has become addicted to meaningless surveys. Over 90 per cent of New Zealand adults consume four or more surveys a week. New Zealand is developing a culture of dependence. Most disturbing of all is the growing binge-mentality, especially among young women.'

SQAC defines a binge as the consumption of five or more surveys at a sitting. In the recent survey, 65 per cent of teenage female respondents admitted to regular bingeing. Typically they would spend up to three hours studying surveys of the sexual and social habits of their peers, and completing magazine questionnaires to see if they were normal.

'An interest in what is normal is normal,' said the SQAC spokesman, 'but when it becomes an obsession it is abnormal. And when three and a quarter out of every five teenage girls in this country are behaving abnormally it is seriously abnormal and a cause for concern. We are particularly concerned about the quarter. But the girls are only mimicking adult behaviour. You can't criticise the young when the adult government is setting the worst possible example.

'The government is addicted to surveys. Without its weekly or even daily fix of public opinion it is incapable of formulating policy. The government leads by following, and young people are following its lead. The whole business smacks of moral decay. With the decline in belief in traditional authorities, people and governments alike are desperate for direction. Surveys appear to offer such direction, but in reality they do no such thing. A recent survey of surveys revealed that 72 per cent of the statistics derived from surveys were meaningless, and that the remaining 28 per cent were pushing a moral agenda.'

When questioned, the spokesman confirmed that the figures of 72 per cent and 28 per cent were among the 72 per cent of survey statistics that were meaningless. 'Which is all the more reason,' he concluded, 'to address the national addiction to surveys. And the change must begin at the top.'

The government has been swift to dismiss SQAC's findings. 'According to a survey,' said the Minister for Policy Development at a hastily convened press conference, 'over 90 per cent of democratic governments around the globe make use of polls, surveys and focus-groups. These things are the tools of office. How do you imagine Tony Blair has succeeded in being such an enduring, charismatic and visionary leader? How could he know what to believe in passionately during any particular week without surveys of the electorate to tell him? SQAC is out of touch with political reality. SQAC fails to understand that the purpose of gaining power is to retain power. Surveys help to achieve that purpose.'

The Survey Manufacturers and Research Marketers of Aotearoa were just as quick to condemn SQAC. 'Every human society has conducted surveys,' stated a SMARMA press release. 'What was it that obliged Mary and Joseph to travel to Bethlehem but a Roman population survey? What was the Domesday Book but an eleventh-century survey of land ownership? Ours is an ancient and honourable industry and SQAC is a bunch of alarmist busybodies. Surveys are just a way for society to look in the mirror. If people didn't want to look in the mirror they wouldn't keep commissioning surveys.'

But an informal survey conducted by this column at the Lava Bar threw a different light on the matter. 'I've consumed a few surveys in my time,' said a sprightly seventy-one-year-old who wished to be known only as Norm, 'and I don't think they've done me any harm. But you shouldn't go taking them seriously. I mean, whenever anyone rings me up to survey my opinion, I consider it an impertinence. So I just tell them the first thing that comes into my head. When I think of some of the stuff I've told those researchers, well, it'd make your eyes water.'

'Off the record,' admitted a SMARMA spokesman, 'truthfulness is our biggest headache. Recently we ran a survey on the subject of responding to surveys and 43 per cent of respondents said that they gave dishonest responses to survey questions either often or very often. We weren't sure whether to believe them. Of the remaining 53 per cent more than half said that they didn't know if they were being dishonest because they didn't have any opinions about responding to surveys. Though some of them thought they might have some opinions after they'd read the results of the survey. But there again, they may have been lying.'

This column has a margin of error of plus or minus two large gins.

Dunbiffin

The mourners came from far and near to gather in Dunbiffin Memorial Hall. A celebrant mounted the stage. 'Ladies and gentleman,' he announced, 'we are gathered here today to mourn Mr Bennett's throwing arm. It died, as we all know, after a long illness bravely borne.

'I am not going to pretend that this arm was a religious arm. It was a throwing arm. It lived to throw. It occupied the present tense. It seized the day, ladies and gentlemen, and having seized it, threw it, preferably at something breakable. That is all the arm did, and that is all I have to say.

'If any of you have something of your own to add, the stage is yours.'

A tin can shambled to the microphone. 'I am a victim of the throwing arm when it was young,' said the can, fingering its dents. 'I was placed on a garden wall and pelted with stones for an entire afternoon. Every time the arm scored a hit, Mr Bennett whooped with delight and set me back on the wall. That arm treated me harshly and I bear the scars to this day, but it did what an arm was meant to do. It was a good arm. May it rest in peace.'

'Thank you, can,' said the celebrant, 'for that moving and generous testimonial.'

Next up was a man in a beret. 'I am a Frenchman,' he said, to the surprise of nobody, unwrapping the skein of garlic from around his neck and hanging it from the lectern. 'I remember the arm well. I used to run a fairground stall near Paris, a sort of coconut shy.

'We French do not throw well. Our sports do not require it. I remember the day when the arm came to my stall on holiday. It found my targets easy to hit. It won prize after prize and Mr Bennett whooped with delight. The arm would have cleaned me out, but then Mr Bennett went too far. "The French all throw like girls," he shouted. His mother dragged him away, laden with coconuts and goldfish in little plastic bags. It was a good strong arm.' The Frenchman stopped to pour himself a glass of wine as thick as arterial blood, then raised it to the crowd. 'Aux arm, citoyens,' he said, and lowered both the glass and himself in a single fluid gesture.

A succession of speakers followed the Frenchman. Seagulls, wicket-keeping gloves, bottles and windows all testified to the arm's exuberant vitality. But it was a wizened little thing, not dissimilar to a walnut in both size and appearance, that spoke the words that went to the nub of things.

'I,' said the walnut-like thing, 'am Mr Bennett's reptilian cortex, the unconscious part of his brain that handles the primitive instincts. I deal in fear, sex, fighting, two-thirds of which Mr Bennett has little aptitude for. But that arm of his,' and here the cortex paused to blow prodigiously into a handkerchief, 'gave me great joy. The raking flat parabola of an accurate throw sent shudders of delight through my ganglions. If I were capable of pity I would pity those who've never known the clean and ringing strike of a stone against a target. Why did throwing thrill me so? An echo of primitive war, perhaps, or an emblem of male potency? I can't say, and in the end I don't care. It was just a pure physical good. It made me happy.'

The reptilian cortex had summed the matter up so well, it seemed that the ceremony was over. But just as the crowd was gathering its things and thinking of refreshments, a hideous figure stood. Dressed in satins and velvets, and with its hair coiffed just so, it slouched to the microphone, burdened with emotion.

Slowly it raised its red-rimmed eyes from the floor. 'Ladies and gentlemen,' it said, in a voice so low that the audience strained to hear, 'my name is Vanity. Masculine Vanity. I don't expect the ladies here to understand, but,' and here his voice cracked, faltered, recovered, 'I killed the arm.'

A gasp ran through the throng.

'Some twenty years ago,' said Vanity, 'I caused the injury that caused the death. A challenge had been issued to find the longest thrower of a cricket ball in these parts. I urged the arm to enter. Each competitor had three throws. With one round remaining, the arm was lying second. Significantly it had already felt pain in its shoulder, but I urged it to throw again. That was the last true throw of its life. The rotator cuff in the arm's shoulder tore like tissue paper.

'Even then, if I'd allowed the arm to go for medical treatment it might have been saved. But no. I, Masculine Vanity, insisted that the damage was trivial, that it would heal. It never healed. Year after year the arm grew weaker. Near the end it could barely lob a cricket ball twenty yards. It was a piteous sight. And I am to blame. I have nothing to say but sorry. I caused a good thing to die. I miss it.' Vanity paused. 'It will never come again,' he said.

There was a silence in Dunbiffin Hall.

The stone has rolled

So a man rang to tell me about this, that and the other. This proved dull, and so did that, but the other was Mick Jagger.

'Isn't he Sir Mick?' I said. 'Like Sir bloody Elton and Sir Paul and Sir Madonna and...'

'No,' he said, 'he's just Mick, of course.'

'Of course,' I said.

'And he's sixty.'

'Sixty?'

'Yes,' he said, 'Mick's sixty. Ha ha.'

'Ha ha,' I said.

'Ha ha,' we said together.

I know what sixty is. Sixty is my grandfather. He died when I was fifteen. For all of those fifteen years he'd been sixty. He was a good man and he'd lived a bit. He'd fought in East Africa in the First World War – though who he fought there, I've no idea – had been a tobacconist and a locksmith, had made his own camera and his own set of chisels. But at sixty he drew the curtains and sat down and turned on the telly and watched horse racing in black and white and smoked roll-ups and kept a goldfinch and sucked imperial mints. Then he upped and died and was burned.

And now Mick's sixty. Mick who was high-octane sexy, strutting and pouting and snogging the microphone, Mick with the mouth like a letter box and the lips like long cushions, Mick who couldn't get no satisfaction, Mick who was the rebellious elder brother, the gifted, girl-getting bad boy, Mick who affronted and offended, whose manner told the sixty-somethings that the world had changed for the worse, that civility had gone, that the jungle was creeping back in, that the young would defer no longer, would never tug a forelock, would insist on being both seen and heard, Mick who was anarchy in jeans, is sixty.

I was never a fan. I could sing along to the easy bits. I'd bellow 'Jumping Jack Flash' and 'Brown Sugar' and 'Hey, hey, you, you get offa my cloud', but I didn't know why Jack jumped or what brown sugar was or what the cloud was or why the interloper wanted onto it. I didn't understand – if, that is, there was anything to understand: I simply knew the noise. The noise was dangerously right and exciting and bad and good, though not enough for me to buy any of it.

The Stones were the Beatles without the saccharine. The Beatles did nice tunes and were pretty and didn't threaten. If daughter brought a Beatle home, Dad just about wouldn't mind. But if daughter hooked up with a Stone, then she wouldn't be coming home. It was time to scour the hotel rooms, ring the cops.

The Stones weren't pretty. Mick's mates were sag-shouldered louts, unwashed smokers. They broke things. And Mick himself was lithe but not beautiful, a svelte but poison-tipped urchin. Lover not husband.

Unlike the Beatles, Mick was angry. Mick would never sing 'Mull of Kintyre'. Mick would never marry a one-legged woman. He did marry, of course, but the woman was built like Chile and had fingernails. She and Mick fought. Rightly. And parted. Rightly.

And now Mick's sixty.

Shakespeare had an image of sixty –

the lean and slippered pantaloon,
With spectacles on nose and pouch on side
His youthful hose well saved, a world too wide
For his shrunk shank.

That's not Mick. Mick's youthful hose still fits him perfectly. I've seen the photos. He's neither shrunk nor fattened. He's got the hair, the teeth. The drugs haven't addled him. Except for a ravine or two, he's got the same fine face.

The Stones still play, sometimes, and the crowds still flock, the same crowds, more or less, as flocked before, but balder, fatter, sagging. Time's speared them in the way it speared my grandfather, is spearing me. But it seems barely to have grazed Mick.

What we want from Mick is the old songs. The new stuff, if there is any new stuff, doesn't interest us. We want our past sung again, or at least what we like to imagine our past was like. That past is Mick's living. He's stuck there, pinned to the dissatisfaction, to the yearning of a post-war generation that didn't aspire to emulate its parents. Our generation was different. We would not grow old.

We proved as different as krill. We grew old. We've quietly slipped into the role of being affronted, affronted by hip-hop, whatever that is, by rap, by drugs and crime and dirty words and lollard youth, by all the things that shocked and affronted our parents. Nothing new there. And that's okay. Time has simply ticked as it has ticked before.

But not for Mick, or at least not for the image of Mick.

'These days, apparently,' said the man on the phone, 'Mick likes cricket.'

'Oh,' I said, and then 'ha ha' and then I thought a bit, and then I said, 'Good.'

Hi art

An Asian man is looking at a cow. The cow is made of corned beef tins. The Asian man is wearing slippers, spectacles and a neutral expression. He seems to find the cow inscrutable.

A horde of infants in uniform bursts round the corner like a shower of ping pong balls. They do not find the cow inscrutable. They scrute it at once. 'It's a cow,' they shout and having shouted they run towards it. 'Stop,' says teacher, and the children come back to her as if attached by elastic. The Asian man looks at the children, looks again at the cow, and pads away in his slippers. The children encircle the cow. 'Don't touch,' says teacher. The children must learn to be serious.

For this is the Christchurch Art Gallery. It cost serious money and it's a serious place.

When I stepped through the gallery's doors I left a nor-wester outside. Looking through the famous wall of wavy glass I see dead leaves skittering across the forecourt, and fat clouds squatting in the mountains, clouds the shape of anvils and the colour of bruises. But I cannot hear the tiny crackle of the skittering leaves, nor feel the warm rush of the wind. The glass turns the world to a silent movie.

Inside, however, it doesn't feel like a movie theatre. It feels like a cathedral. As in a cathedral there is a sense of sanctuary and reverence. And as in a cathedral, everything's dwarfed by the height of the roof. The people creep on hushed feet. This is the high house of high culture.

It takes a while to find the paintings. The first to confront me is the well known daub of the Otira River by Van der Velden. From a distance it looks large and gloomy. From close up it looks clumsy and gloomy, no better to my eye than the sort of amateur exhibition you see on pegboards in a shopping mall. The informative plaque tells me that it reflects the nineteenth-century fad for the sublime. I fail to see sublimity. I see more skill in, and spend more time with, some paintings of nineteenth-century Lyttelton. They are paintings of the precise and literal sort that photography and the twentieth century skewered.

Around the corner I discover a Rembrandt portrait. You can't mistake a Rembrandt portrait – black background, high shafts of light and a subject whose face has been cudgelled by time. Nevertheless I feel smug to have recognised it. I stand a while to admire its moody genius, then read the informative plaque. It tells me that this Rembrandt is by Van der Velden. The moody genius wilts a little.

In half an hour of wandering the gallery I travel a hundred years, from the traditional comforts of the nineteenth century to the discomforts of the twentieth, from the self-effacing craft of Goldie to the self-obsessed anguish of McCahon. I prefer Goldie.

Big black beetles and crude red shapes are fixed to a wall. 'By creating silhouettes,' says the informative plaque, 'Killeen drains the pieces of their individuality and detail so they exist somewhere between abstraction and realism.'

Actually my notes are a scrawl and the last word may not have been realism. But you could replace it with almost any abstract noun.

What you say about art doesn't matter. It matters only that you have something to say. It's like knowing the words of the church service in Latin. You become an insider. You join the club.

I stand a while to listen to a guide. She is explaining to a group of lunchable women a painting by Peter Robinson that doesn't seem to me to need much explaining. The painting consists of advice on how to con people into thinking you're a serious artist.

In a downstairs gallery a lot of ordinary seashells are laid in patterns on the floor. This 'art practice,' says the informative plaque, 'is characterised by an intense and explorative approach to the natural environment'. What the plaque fails to add is that my dogs are also characterised by an intense and explorative approach to the natural environment, only they don't call it an art practice. They call it going for a walk.

But I don't mean to carp. What I or the critics or the curators say about the art doesn't matter much. Even the art itself doesn't matter much. What matters is that this place exists, that it is a refuge from the wind, a place where a man in slippers can stand seriously in front of a metal cow for as long as he likes. It's a temple, and we need temples. Even if our faith is misplaced, it still serves the need.

At the foot of the great glass wall there's a neat architectural touch. Comma-shaped pools of water appear to pass beneath the wall, so that half of each pool lies inside the building and half in the open air. The water outside is rippled by the wind and pocked with the first drops of coming rain. But inside the building the water is a mirror: reflective, untroubled, a still life.

Five and a half intimates

A woman rang me. She was organising a book festival. Would I run a workshop, she said. No, I said.

I said that I had done workshops and found that I did all the work. My workshops were lectures.

Well then, she said, would I like to give a lecture? I said I would be happy to talk about my favourite books. She said that would be dandy. I give the talk this evening. Last night I thought I should do something about it.

By counting the books on a shelf and then multiplying by the number of my shelves, I estimated that I own 1200 books. I've read almost all of them, but I'll read very few of them again. I keep them because I think they make me look clever. They also insulate the house.

I toured the shelves with a notebook, writing down the names of favourite authors. My shelves are roughly alphabetical. By the time I'd reached 'L' I'd filled two pages. 'L' was particularly fruitful: Lanchester, Larkin, Harper Lee, Laurie Lee, Levi, Levin, Lively, Lodge… I made a cup of coffee, sat on the dirty sofa, thought a bit, looked at my list and scrunched it. It was not a list of my favourite authors. It was a list of authors I liked, like an address book. What I wanted was the intimates.

Just as you have countless acquaintances, several friends, but only a very few people that you would run to in times of trouble, so it is with authors. There are a few, a very few, whose books I return to time and again. Just to think of reading them is to feel a sense of indulgence, like sinking into a hot bath of milk. Books as comfort in a spiky world. Books as succour.

I started a new list. I included only the books I'd read at least three times. In the end I had a dozen. I asked myself who the true lovers were, the writers I would like to curl with on the dirty sofa that very minute, and deep in whose words I would happily spend the day. I culled more from my dozen, each with a pang. I was left with those I just could not cross out. There were five and a half of them.

The five were Evelyn Waugh, Philip Larkin, Albert Camus, William Shakespeare, Laurie Lee. The half was Thomas Hardy.

I do not pretend they are the best five and half authors in the world. Shakespeare is the best five and a half authors in the world. Shakespeare is the best hundred and five and a half authors.

Of the others, Waugh was a vicious bigot, Larkin a misery, Camus a poseur, Lee a romantic and Hardy a clumsy doomster.

They're all men and they're all dead. Five were English, one French. But what counts, I think, is that I first read each of them in my late teens. That's the volatile age, the age of greatest intensity. Time is never so rich again. It's the age when the fledgling bird shuffles onto the branch and wonders if it can fly.

None of these authors taught me. None of them showed me anything new. Rather they coupled with my mind. Each fitted a bit of my head like a plug in a socket. Each gave words to something I had sensed, apart from Shakey, who gave words to everything I had sensed.

In *Decline and Fall*, Waugh showed me a hard and glittering world of knaves and suckers, a world where the amoral did things and the nice suffered the consequences. And he made me laugh. In the first half of *Brideshead Revisited* he drowned me in love like honey. In the second half he didn't convert me to Catholicism.

I lived in the suburbs. Larkin showed me the suburbs. He stripped off the comforts to reveal a skeleton of desperation. I had sensed that desperation. To see it clear thrilled me. It relieved the desperation.

Camus showed me random. He showed me that things happened only because they happened. There is no thread. I had already sensed that all the threads were false. Camus gave me the courage to believe my disbelief.

Laurie Lee, well, he went walking in Spain. And though I doubt the detail of the book – he wrote it almost twenty years after the event – he did the job in words so vivid that they seared my mind. And from those words I reaped a sense of coloured purposelessness, of beauty in the arbitrary sideshows of the everyday. I still suspect him of romanticism, but to cross him off would be to deny the way his words seduced me then and still seduce me now.

Hardy made me cry. And Shakespeare, well, he made me wonder how anyone since has found anything to say.

I'm looking forward to giving the lecture. It will be the purest self-indulgence. If no one comes to listen to it, I shall give it to the empty chairs.

McFilm

I knew there was something wrong with film as a medium and Hollywood as culture when I was taken to see *101 Dalmatians* at the age of eight. Twenty minutes into the film I erupted screaming from my seat, ran home, grabbed the family dog, barricaded myself under the bed and refused to emerge until puberty. Apart, that is, from nipping out at the age of eleven to see *Where Eagles Dare* twice. I went the second time only to confirm that it was as bad as it had seemed the first time. It was.

Offhand I can think of only three films I've seen that I would happily see again: *Cabaret, My Life as a Dog* (which has little to do with dogs) and *If.*

If tells the story of a revolution at a crusty boarding school. I once tried to rent *If* when I was teaching in a similarly crusty boarding school in Canada. Most of the little darlings I was teaching were merely shoppers in embryo, salivating at the prospect of acquiring the latest hugely advertised gewgaw that the industrial complex had cooked up to shrivel their tiny minds. I thought *If* might shake one or two of them at the roots of their consumerist complacency.

Fat chance twice over. First, a fat chance of undoing a dozen years of televisual brainwashing. Even back then, Canada had the biggest shopping mall in the world, and liked to boast about it. It was somewhere in Alberta. Maybe it *was* Alberta. And second, a fat chance of actually finding a copy of *If*.

At the local video store I was offered 3000 indistinguishable Hollywood megabusters starring good old Sly or Arnie acting the Neanderthal with hi-tech weaponry and a death-per-minute rating to eclipse the Battle of the Somme.

But that's film for you. Film does shallow emotive nonsense splendidly. What it doesn't do is serious thoughtful sense.

Most film is ephemeral, superficial pap, a sort of visual Prozac. It's eye-candy, bereft of substance. The reason for this poverty is that film struggles to render complex interior humanity. That's the domain of literary fiction. But literary fiction doesn't stand a hope against film. It asks too much work of the reader. The future is six-gun Arnie and you're welcome to him. If you want me I'll be up the hill in a cave reading Jonathan Franzen.

Of course some films do try to do the stuff that literature does. Most of them fail. You get twee versions of Jane Austen with lawns and horses and muslin dresses with the waistline just below the bust so the women all look like shuttlecocks. What you don't get is waspish old Jane sticking the knife into her gargoyle creations.

Or else you get dark and moody art house cinema filmed on the fiord-ravaged coast of Norway where women with blow-drier hair stand on cliff tops and look longingly at seagulls. And as you crane to read the semi-literate subtitles you are surrounded by such awful film buffs braying about symbolism in their polo-neck sweaters that you half hope for Arnie to wander in, grunt and mow them down while oiling his biceps.

And then there's the fantasy. Cinema has always done fantasy.

There's the romantic fantasy stuff to gratify the yearning breasts of disappointed women, stuff in which Cary Grant, or his brother Hugh, arrives with immaculate grooming to lay the heroine tenderly amid the cool sheets of paradise. Then there's the adventure fantasy in which Indiana Tarzan does unlikely things to bad people who want to do unspeakable things to him. And increasingly there's the altogether elsewhere fantasy like *Lord of the Rings*. Harmless stuff in its way, a sort of Wombles with blood, but hardly a pinnacle of cultural achievement. Not that that bothers the devotees who are flocking to New Zealand with their little knapsacks and their locations guide and their cheese and pickle sandwiches to make reverential pilgrimages to the spot of turf out the back of Ashburton where Dopo drew his enchanted sword and slew the mighty Torpor, leader of the Woks.

Nor does it bother the government. There's money in those knapsacks. And so our leaders are now offering tax breaks to Hollywood. As a result it seems likely that New Zealand will stop being Middle Earth and will become the set for *The Lion, the Witch and the Infantile Regression Syndrome*, and who knows what other barren little entertainments to take our minds off an overpopulated planet.

I never did find *If*. After traipsing round Video Hut and McVideo and Kentucky Fried Video and finding nothing but multiple copies of the same mindless guff, I went home and used the phone. The first three stores I rang had never heard of *If*. The girl in the fourth store asked me to repeat the title. And then she asked me to spell it.

My last hope was an outfit called Red Hot Videos. 'Have you,' I asked down the phone, 'by any chance, got a copy of a film made in the sixties called *If*?'

'Hold on,' said the man. He returned a minute later. 'Sorry, no,' he said, 'but we have got one called *F*. Will that do?'

Arachnametaphor

The spider had spun a web across my wing-mirror. Presumably it hoped to catch female flies.

I admire spiders. I admire the way they bungy gently from ceiling to floor. And I admire even more the way they reverse bungy to the ceiling by eating the rope. I admire the way they torture flies. (I am soft on animals but flies don't count. I like the thought of a fly becoming soup while retaining consciousness.) I admire the static trawlers that are spider webs. And I particularly admire the way non-venomous spiders inspire terror in human beings 3 billion times their size.

I taught a child who went on to become an All Black. If there was a spider in the classroom this child left the classroom. He left it at a speed that later served him well. He scattered desks like would-be tacklers. His exits were so memorable it was worth importing spiders specially.

I am not an arachnophobe. But neither am I an arachnophile. I share with most of the population, it seems, an arachnoslightuneasiness. Small spiders do not trouble me. Indeed they are welcome in my house because of our shared enmity to flies. If I spot a spider the size of a ten-cent piece on my bedroom ceiling, I blow it a kiss, wish it sweet dreams, turn off the light and sleep the deep sleep of a man without worries. But if the spider is the size of a fifty-cent piece and possessed of legs that arch like the McDonald's logo, then I will rise from my virgin bachelor sheets and capture the thing in a glass and transport it to the garden at arm's length with a slightly wrinkled nose – my own, that is, not the spider's, whose nose I never remember to study – and I will toss it well away from me and scamper back and shut the door behind me and hope the spider doesn't know how to work the cat flap.

The spider on the wing mirror was a twenty-cent piece spider. As I reversed down the drive its value shrank. By the time I was on the open road and heading for the beach with the dogs in the back and a song on my lips, the spider had suffered serious inflation. Diameter-wise it was worth less than five cents. It had appraised the situation and gathered itself into a ball.

Though actually I doubt that it did much appraising. The events were beyond a spider's appraising scope. The beast had gone to bed on the wing mirror confident that it had found somewhere solid to hang up its hat for a while. Then it awoke to find that somewhere bowling along the open road. It was as if I had awoken to find the whole of Lyttelton jogging to Sydney. And if that were to occur I expect that, like the spider, I would curl into a ball and whimper. Not of course that I could tell whether the spider was whimpering. The window between us acted as a barrier to sound. And it was too cool a morning to wind it down to study the audible grief of a spider.

Rolling into a ball as a form of defence is a common tactic and a good one. Spiders, woodlice and people being kicked do it. Hedgehogs do it particularly well, whether they're being kicked or, as is now common in these parts, being hunted by my new dingbat of a dog. But it takes a lot to dissuade a dingbat. The dog picks up the coiled hedgehog, brings it to me in triumph and looks up at me with eyes beseeching praise, tail going like a flag in a gale and tongue gently dripping blood. When I lean down to congratulate the dog on his devoted stupidity, I sometimes hear the tightly curled hedgehog giggling.

I am confident the wing-mirror spider wasn't giggling. It was too busy clinging with eight legs. Aerodynamically a sphere is a better shape than a spider's usual posture, but it still can't be a doddle to retain a grip at 80 kilometres an hour when your usual top speed is 80 metres a day. But though its web went west, the spider hung on.

The dogs and I frolicked on the beach for an hour. When we came back the spider was still on the mirror. I drove home gently, believing the spider had been through enough for one day.

All that was yesterday. This morning when I went out with the dog to fetch the newspaper, I noted that the spider was still on the wing mirror. Indeed it had recovered sufficiently from its trauma to spin itself another web, and all without so much as a single counselling session.

So what? Well, I am tempted to see the spider as a metaphor. For what? For everything. Go about your business, it suggests. You will make monumental errors, like setting up house on a swift-moving mirror, but don't let the fear of error dissuade you. When things go wrong, as they will, hang on tight. The storm will pass. And when it's passed, just start again. That's all.

But I shall resist the temptation of metaphor. Partly because it's only a spider. But mainly because on my way back up the drive with the paper, I killed it.

Treehog

There's a class of people I constantly meet who imply that the world is an arbitrary place. When confronted with an oddity, they chuckle and say, 'Well I never, there's a first time for everything', looking all the while as if they were the offspring of Ernest Rutherford and Immanuel Kant and had pierced to the heart of a random universe.

So ubiquitous are these people that if I were chained to the wall of a Mexican dungeon accompanied only by a tame green budgerigar that happened to have a thermonuclear device strapped to its leg, a thermonuclear device furthermore that was primed to detonate in thirty seconds, I would fully expect some dingbat to appear at the barred window, cast an eye over the situation and say, 'Well I never, there's a first time for everything.'

'No there bloody well isn't,' I'd scream, at which point, with any luck, the budgerigar would fly through the window and chase the platitudinous dork in the hope of pecking his eyes out. Thirty seconds later the detonation would rattle the dungeon walls sufficiently to loosen the manacles, thus permitting me to escape ahead of the mushroom cloud, holding a handkerchief to my nose and thinking warm thoughts about the budgerigar. Unlikely? Perhaps, but then there's a first time for everything.

Only, of course, there isn't. The world isn't that arbitrary. To give just one example, there will never be a first time for me to attend an aromatherapy class.

And yet, if you had asked me yesterday whether there would be a first time for me to have a hedgehog stuck up a kowhai tree in my garden, I would have said no. But right now there's a hedgehog stuck up a kowhai tree in my garden. And it presents me with a choice. I can either leave the hedgehog where it is, or I can grab an extension ladder and a pair of oven mitts and launch into a hedgehog variation of the fireman-and-stuck-cat routine that has brought joy to millions of spectators but to few cats.

The hedgehog's predicament is all my fault. I tossed the thing off the deck. But I didn't expect it to get stuck in the tree. Rather I expected it to tumble through the branches in the manner of a pinball in an old-fashioned arcade machine, and then to drop onto the dandelions below, shaken but unharmed.

Unfortunately I tossed hurriedly and the hedgehog lodged in a fork in the kowhai. I tossed hurriedly because my dog was coming.

He's a young dog and passionately fond of hedgehogs and he rarely looks before he leaps. So I was afraid that if he saw the hedgehog flying over the edge of the deck he would leap after it.

Thirty kilos of labrador would not tumble through the branches in the manner of a pinball in an arcade machine. Rather they would accelerate through the branches in the manner of an old-fashioned East German female athlete doing the hurdles. These women were so primed with synthetic testosterone that when they did the hurdles they really did the hurdles. Peasants used to follow them to collect the kindling.

So, not wanting my dog to leap off the deck, crash through the branches and land on the dandelions with a thud that would keep the vet in clover, I tossed the hedgehog with excessive haste and turned away, whistling a nonchalant tune as I did so in a bid to impersonate a man who is just strolling on his deck to enjoy the warmth of the evening and who has never so much as heard of hedgehogs, let alone just tossed one away.

The dog was not convinced. He knew there had been a hedgehog on the deck because he'd just put it there himself.

I've given up trying to wrestle hedgehogs from this dog. What I do instead is to make him stay outside on the deck with the hedgehog while I take my old dog inside and feed her. Young dog watches through the window until food-greed overcomes hedgehog-greed. He then drops the hedgehog, sprints round the back and enters through the dog door. Meanwhile I slip out the deck door and liberate the hedgehog before the dog wakes up to the deception.

So what I have now is a puzzled dog, though it's not half as puzzled as the hedgehog's going to be when it unfurls itself. Its name suggests that it may be familiar with hedges, but I doubt that any hedgehog in history has found itself 6 metres up a tree and comprehensively forked. The poor thing will be terrified. It will twitch and gibber and break into sweats and it may then do something unwise and possibly fatal.

All of which urges me to go and rescue it but I haven't got an extension ladder. My neighbour has, but he and I have never actually spoken. It's not that there's bad blood between us. We just both prefer to look before we leap.

Nevertheless I'm now going round to knock on his door and ask to borrow his ladder. And if, when I explain why I want it, he doesn't chuckle and say with an air of bogus sagacity, 'Well I never, there's a first time for everything', I'll join an aromatherapy class.

Mean

I gather that the World Trade Organisation has held 'meaningful discussions'. That's good to know. But what does meaningful mean in this context, and in particular what does it mean for you and me? These are the questions I mean to answer by means of this column.

In the first place, and to the relief of everyone, the meaningful discussions appear to mean that the Doha Round is still alive. Doha, of course, doesn't mean Doha. Doha means Cancun. But if the meaningful discussions mean what they appear to mean, then it won't be long before Doha stops meaning Cancun and starts meaning somewhere else.

What will that mean for somewhere else? Well, first off, it will mean the gravy train chugging into town. Of course the gravy train means neither gravy nor a train. What it means is a free lunch, and, as we all know, a free lunch means the opposite of a free lunch. It means an expensive breakfast, an expensive lunch, an expensive dinner and several expensive cocktails with cherries in, plus a snack from the amusingly expensive minibar, all of it paid for by someone else. And someone else, ladies and gentlemen, means the taxpayer. And the taxpayer means you and me.

So I think we're entitled to know who exactly will be eating the free lunch that you and I have paid for. And it's a question I mean to answer in a manner that will leave you in no doubt of my meaning. The suits, ladies and gentlemen, the suits will be eating our lunch.

Of course, suits doesn't mean suits. Suits means the men and women who wear suits, or rather the men who wear suits and the women who would wear suits if they were men. But because they're not men they wear trouser suits instead of suits. A trouser suit means a pair of trousers and a jacket, as opposed to a suit, which means a pair of trousers and a jacket. If that distinction means nothing to you, forget it. I'm not here to quibble about meanings.

So, when I say suits I mean the men and women who represent their countries at the World Trade Organisation. These men and women have been chosen by the elected governments of their respective countries, chosen, in other words, by the chosen, with the word chosen in that last phrase having two slightly different meanings. (I am excluding for the sake of simplicity the non-democratic countries. In their case the suits means the people chosen by the unchosen or the self-chosen.)

So, having clarified those meanings, what does it all mean? Let's start with the meaning of the World Trade Organisation itself. World obviously means world. Trade, equally obviously, means the rules that restrict trade. And organisation means the forum in which they have meaningful talks about free trade.

Free trade means different things to different countries. The United States of America is a champion of free trade, by which it means subsidising its own farmers. New Zealand is also a champion of free trade, by which it means not subsidising its own farmers. What does this mean? This means a need for meaningful discussions.

But meaningfulness is not only to be found inside the World Trade Organisation. There is plenty of meaningfulness to be found outside it. Because any meeting of the World Trade Organisation invariably means protesters.

Protesters mean to break into the meaningful discussions that the World Trade Organisation is holding. What the protesters are protesting about is globalisation, and we all know what globalisation means. Globalisation means McDonald's. Globalisation means big American corporations exploiting people by selling them things they want.

The protesters are on the side of the poor countries. They believe that the World Trade Organisation means to destroy the traditional life of those poor countries. But it is important to note that by protesters I do not mean the people who actually lead that traditional life. Those people are far too poor to travel to Cancun to protest.

It is not clear what the protesters mean to do if they manage to break into the meaningful discussions. But they never do manage to break in, because between the protesters and the World Trade Organisation stand the riot police. The riot police mean business.

Of course, business used in this sense does not mean business. The business of the riot police means hitting protesters with sticks so that the World Trade Organisation can carry on its business. Not that business in this sense means business either. The business of the World Trade Organisation means holding meaningful discussions.

The real meaning of the word business is industry. Industry means making things to sell, which means trade. Business, in other words, consists of organisations that exist in the world to trade. And it is essential to understand that organisations that exist in the world to trade are not represented at the World Trade Organisation. It's none of their business.

I hope you have found this discussion meaningful. If you wish for more I would advise you to acquire a copy of *The Meaning of Meaning* by I. A. Richards, a pioneer in the study of semantics and a keen amateur auto-proctologist.

Dinnerhoea

Fourteen years ago I was twice his age but now I'm not. I still don't understand how that could be, which was why I taught him English instead of Maths.

When I say I taught him English, I wouldn't want you to imagine that I taught him any, well, English. By the time I got to stand in front of the little brute, he was sixteen years old and already spoke and wrote the language. It was like being plonked in front of Einstein and being told you had a year to train him to use a calculator. All that was required of me was a bit of show-offery like spelling diarrhoea.

I like diarrhoea. The word has a grisly onomatopoeic beauty. I also like onomatopoeic. And I despise the way Americans take the 'o' out of diarrhoea, thereby destroying the diphthong. I like the word diphthong, too, though I bet the Yanks take the first 'h' out of it, thereby turning the language from a rich thick beer into a Miller's Bloody Lite.

And as for the Simplified Spelling nutters who want to make English into some sort of safe phonetic shopping mall, well, I wish them nothing less than a bowt of diareya so spektakyular and protrakted that thay grone til there dipfongs ake. Then perhaps they might understand that the majestic complexity of English spelling is nothing more nor less than a hurdles race in which the first hurdle is set at dog and the last at diarrhoea, and the hurdle at which any competitor falls is as sure a guide to their moral worth as I know.

And don't give me any nonsense about dyslexia. The English language is a hard master, not given to handkerchiefs, hugs or counselling, as evidenced by the delicious difficulty of spelling dyslexia, not to mention the 's' in lisp, though I now find that I have mentioned it. Nor do I want to hear any bleating about spellchecks. I've just run the spellcheck over this. It highlighted 'spellcheck' because the greedy little programme wanted to turn itself into two words, which it doesn't deserve and isn't going to get so long as I'm in charge, and it also highlighted the jokes. Spellchecks don't get jokes. Their little binary chips get as flustered as Bill Gates confronted by a piece of poetry.

Anyway the half-my-age lad, who is now neither of those things, wants to go out to dinner. Tonight. It was his idea. He sent me an email out of that famously unpredictable colour, the blue. Let's do dinner, he said, which is the sort of English I like a lot.

He was a clever child. He was also funny. Of course, I wasn't having any of that being funny stuff in my classroom, where it was my job to be funny and his job to laugh and to learn how to spell diarrhoea.

But he was funny in his essays. Very few children are funny in their essays, or at least very few are funny when they try to be. He even wrote funny stuff about Shakespeare. Shakespeare would have liked funny stuff about Shakespeare more than he would have liked earnest stuff about Shakespeare.

Anyway this lad is still writing funny essays and they are being published and now he wants to go for dinner. I am looking forward to it, which is absurd because I know exactly how it will be. We will meet in the bar and we will shake hands and he will think but not say how bald I have grown (though grown seems the opposite of the correct verb) and my side of the conversation will run like this:

Hello… Oh, thank you. A beer… No, anything but a Miller's Lite, actually… Cheers. So, er well, tell me, what have you been, sort of, you know, up to, since I last, well, saw you?… I see… Oh really. Did you like Peru?… I see. Ha ha … Oh, really. And did you like Cambodia?… I see, really. Would you care for another?… Right, where were we? Hindustan, wasn't it?… Oh, that's right, Glasgow… Oh really, did she? Gosh … And what happened to the goat? … What, me? Nothing to tell really. One of my dogs died. That's about it, I think… No, I don't. Twenty years teaching is more than enough for anyone… No, I don't remember him… No, I don't remember him… No, I don't remember him… Well, actually I was a bit afraid of you, too… No, really, I was… Nice of you to say that, but it isn't true… No, I mean it, I didn't teach you a thing… Okay, tell me one thing I actually taught you… Brilliant. I'd forgotten about that. Did you know the Yanks leave the 'o' out?… Oh, did I? Let's have a lot more drinks.

Ridiculously excited

I have bought a new television. It is the third television of my life and I am waiting for it to arrive now. I am ridiculously excited.

When I bought my first television I was also ridiculously excited. That television was old and cheap and the size of a small horse. I was excited by its bigness. But when I got it home its bigness embarrassed me. I tried to disguise that bigness by putting a pot plant on it. I hoped people would say, 'What a nice pot plant.' They didn't. They said, 'What a big television. Oh, and your pot plant's dying.'

Watering a plant is not gratifying. When you feed a dog it wags its tail. When you buy a man a drink he wags his tail too. But when you water a plant it does nothing. So I generally forget to. And when I do remember, I tend to drown the thing.

I have watched many plants die and it is not a spectacular process. But I have watched only one television die, my horse-sized one. Its death wasn't a process but it was spectacular. It happened when I watered the plant. The bang made the cat disappear for a week. When the smoke cleared the plant seemed fine.

My second television was brand-new, with a remote control.

I was ridiculously excited by it. And because my first telly was embarrassingly big I replaced it with a dwarf one. I hoped people would say, 'My word, what a tiny television. You must be a terribly cerebral person with no time for the lurid gewgaws of contemporary trash culture.' They didn't. They said, 'Why don't you get a decent-sized television?'

Then last year my tiny telly shrank. I found that during a rugby match I could no longer read the score in the corner of the screen. Of course that's not a problem when England are playing because you know they will be winning, but for other games it's annoying.

Then last week a woman visited me. She picked up my remote control. 'This is filthy,' she said. I chose not to argue.

The woman went to the kitchen and fetched one of those squirty things that turns cheap detergent into excitingly expensive detergent. She squirted the remote control a few times and rubbed it till it gleamed like an ornament. Which was fortunate because the remote control had become an ornament.

Once you've had a remote control it's tedious not to have one. It's like having your dog go deaf.

So I went shopping and I struck it lucky. I wasn't served by any ordinary sales person. I was served by a sales consultant. He was about nineteen and he had what may have been Marmite on his shirt.

I asked him why one of the televisions was a lot cheaper than the others. He said it didn't have a wide screen or a flat screen. Apparently a wide screen lets you see what's going on at the edges of movies and a flat screen lets you watch from an oblique angle. I said I was an old-fashioned type. I liked the stuff in the middle of movies and I tended to sit square on to the screen. 'Then that's the telly for you,' he said. You can see why he became a consultant so young.

I shop in the same way as I water plants. I don't do it often but when I do I tend to do lots of it quickly. This is partly because once I have forced myself into a shop I feel like a terrier in a barrel of rats. But it is also because I imagine that if I do a lot of shopping now, I won't have to do any more for a long time. So along with a television I bought a video player and a wall bracket to support them both.

I asked if the wall bracket was easy to assemble. The consultant said it was a piece of cake.

Pieces of cake don't normally come with instructions. Nor did the wall bracket. Instead it came with a list of the 7000 bits that were in the box. The list was helpfully translated into six languages. I was pleased to learn that the German for domed shakeproof nut is gesicherte hutmutter. It sounds like a dried scoutmistress.

But there was also a set of easy-to-follow diagrams which enabled me to assemble the thing and fix it rigidly to the wall before you could say two broken drill bits, quite a lot of blood and the whole of one Sunday.

But now I'm sitting with my scoutmistresses unshakeably fixed and I am looking out for the television delivery man with a sense of ridiculous excitement. I particularly look forward to discovering what new form of disappointment awaits me.

SOBS

'Miss Biltong,' says the headmaster, leading us down a corridor that smells of disinfectant and caged hope and gym shoes, 'is the longest-serving teacher at SOBS. Nevertheless she is… I'm sorry? Oh, of course, silly of me. SOBS is the School of Business Speak. Living as I do within the cloistered calm of SOBS, I find it easy to forget that not everybody in this world is a FOTA.

'Anyway, as I was saying, Miss Biltong is… I'm sorry? Oh, there I go again. Fan of the Acronym. I do apologise. But, as I was saying, I don't think I would be exaggerating to say that Miss Biltong's influence stretches into every boardroom in the country. Her catechisms of business language are based on an idea by Flann O'Brien, an Irish writer, who filched the idea himself from the Catholic church. But the content of Miss Biltong's catechisms is all her own. Once learned, those catechisms are never forgotten. Give Miss Biltong a company director at the age of seven, and he is hers for life.'

The headmaster pauses at a classroom door, and gestures at the honours boards above it. In the faded gold lettering I recognise the names of some of this country's most distinguished captains of industry.

'I believe,' says the headmaster, his ear to the door, 'that we are in luck. Miss Biltong is just beginning a catechism class.'

Through the door comes a firm but elderly female voice, intoning a greeting in a sing-song pattern familiar to all who have suffered through primary school.

'Good morning, human resources,' says the voice.

'Good morning, Miss Biltong,' comes the sing-song echo.

The headmaster opens the door sufficiently for us to file into the back of the room. A woman of mature years, to whom time has not been kind, stands before a class of children. They have the bright eyes of the young, she the tweed skirt of the old. Her hair is done in a bun. She seems frail but authoritative.

'So Theresa,' says Miss Biltong, the light glinting from her steel-framed spectacles, 'choose a number.'

'Twenty-seven, Miss Biltong.'

'Splendid. Business Language Catechism 27 it is. Are we all ready?'

'Yes, Miss Biltong.'

'When you become company directors, will you be paid?'

'No, we shall receive remuneration.'

'How does remuneration relate to wages?'

'Very nicely.'

'Does your company ever spend a lot of money?'

'No, it has a capital expenditure programme.'

'Is it a meaningless capital expenditure programme?'

'No, it is a significant capital expenditure programme.'

'By what nautical metaphor do you undertake this significant capital expenditure programme?'

'We embark on it.'

'What's the time?'

'An obsolete word for time-frame.'

'What are checks?'

'The first half of balances.'

'What's the difference between… Yes Stephen, what is it?'

'May I be excused, Miss?'

'Stephen, Stephen, Stephen, when will you learn? Can anyone help Stephen? Yes, Theresa?'

'Stephen hopes to achieve a leaner structure by natural wastage.'

'Very good, Theresa. And Stephen, the answer's no. We have a catechism to complete. So, what's the difference between checks and balances?'

'No one knows.'

'Do we ever pay off debt?'

'No, we don't.'

'What age-related activity do we apply to it?'

'We retire it.'

'What redundant phrase can we affix to the end of every sentence?'

'Going forward.'

'How often should we use the term robust, going forward?'

'As often as possible without reference to its meaning.'

'Do businesses expand?'

'No, we grow them.'

'What is it now, Stephen?'

'Please Miss Biltong, I've think I've achieved a leaner structure by natural wastage, going forward.'

'Has the market bottomed out, Stephen?'

'Robustly, Miss.'

'Very well, my little human resources, this seems an appropriate moment to pause for morning break. You may use the level playing field, but, please, no one is to move the goalposts. And no climbing on the regulatory framework. Is that understood?'

'Yes, Miss Biltong.'

'You may go.'

The happy children scamper from the classroom and the head-master turns to us with a look of gratification.

'As you can see, gentlemen,' he says, 'there is hardly a company report written in this country that does not owe something to Miss Biltong. QED, I believe.'

Necks, please

I've got an inexplicable bad neck. Went to sleep last night with a neck so pliant I had ostriches asking me my secret, but awoke this Sunday morning with a neck like a crankshaft – not that I quite know what a crankshaft is, but if it's as inflexible and knobbly as I imagine it to be, then it's bang right. Perhaps I should ring an osteopath – not that I quite know what an osteopath is either.

And anyway I expect osteopaths play golf on Sunday, swinging their spine-straight clubs with such smug rubberiness that they drum up custom even on the Sabbath – not that I'm quite sure what the Sabbath is, since Jews, I believe, think it's Saturday, Gentiles Sunday, and teenagers the name of a rock group. I could look it up, I suppose, along with crankshaft and osteopath, but the dictionary's down there to my right and I'm up here at my desk nursing my neck, and the fear of pain beats the thirst for knowledge. Injury does that. The world shrinks to the point of pain and nothing else matters.

By swivelling my eyes, which is the only form of exercise I feel up to, I can see birds with irritatingly good necks. Greenfinches are clinging to the seed bell I thoughtfully hang for them, and jabbing at it with necks all lissome and enviable. They keep their balance by fluttering one wing. I didn't realise birds could move their wings independently, although if you think about it, which I'm doing for the first time, it makes sense. I mean, if you wave your right arm, the left one doesn't flap in sympathy. It would make carpentry tricky.

Anyway I can't remember ever seeing a bird with a crook neck, though I've seen plenty with crooked necks, most notable among which are shags, herons and bitterns. Shags fold their necks into an 'S' when roosting, but straighten them in flight. Herons do the opposite. Bitterns, meanwhile, whose necks are habitually as crooked as snakes, stick them vertically into the air whenever they sense danger. The idea, apparently, is that they then resemble reeds. At which point the prowling predator says, 'Well, bugger me. Could have sworn there was a bittern round here but no, nothing but reeds. Guess I'll just go off to the beach and get myself a shag.'

Bitterns are rare birds and, to be frank, I'm not surprised. The reed-imitation gambit doesn't seem like a winner to me. Though I suppose it is just possible that bitterns are actually the most abundant birds in the world and what you and I imagine to be reed beds are in fact enormous flocks of bitterns. In which case, I suppose, bitterns may have been used over the years to thatch cottages, which is a picturesque notion so long as the bitterns didn't suddenly and collectively decide to migrate – not that I actually know whether bitterns migrate. I could look it up, of course, but the bird book's next to the dictionary.

Anyway I wouldn't make a very good bittern this morning. While mooching through the reed bed in search of a frog to spear for Sunday lunch, I'd sense the presence of a predator, a polecat, say – not that I'm quite sure what a polecat is – and I'd switch into reed mode. The polecat would catch the creaking of vertebrae, spot the reed with a wince on its face and a suspiciously feathered stem, and suddenly, well, once bitten no bittern, and one less bit of thatching for your cottage. Which perhaps explains why I've never seen any sort of bird with a crook neck. Though a bloke I met yesterday told me he once saw a duck pretending to be crippled. It was limping around begging bread from sympathetic children. But when the bread ran out, it straightened up and walked off a well duck. Good on it, I say, in this dog eat dog world, not, as it happens, that I've ever seen a dog eat a dog.

But I have seen chickens eat chicken. I used sometimes to collect a bucket of leftovers from the Volcano and bring it back for my chooks. They'd dive into the swill with gusto, flinging fish and peas and anchovies over their shoulders as they frantically rummaged for any morsel of their own kind. Not liking to think I had a backyard of clucking cannibals, I've stopped bringing them leftovers, but I've since discovered that chooks aren't choosy carnivores.

Only this week my dog threw up after chewing her morning cow bone. Dogs are supposed to return to their own vomit but Jessie never got a chance. Before you could say nausea, the gutsiest of my chooks had strutted up and was picking through … well, you don't need the details.

Which reminds me that I haven't got any food in the fridge which means that I'm going to have to go to the shops which means that I'm going to have to reverse out of the drive. And since my chances of twisting my neck to look over my shoulder when reversing are about as high as a bittern's chances of being mistaken for a reed, perhaps I should just sit in my front garden looking woebegone and hope that some sympathetic children pass by on their way to the duck pond, not that we've actually got a duck pond round here. Or many sympathetic children. It's all, to be frank, a pain in the neck.

Tomorrow is a foreign country

Queen's Birthday Weekend and I had an epiphany – although epiphany seems too long a word to describe something that lasted only a second or two. It was more of an epiph.

I was happy and with a novelist, which is a rare combination. It's not that I'm seldom happy, but rather that I seldom consort with writers. They're a gruesome bunch, whining self-obsessives most of them, with awful armpits.

Actually one of my favourite daydreams is writer hunting. In the dream I tote a magnum and ride a horse. The writer totes nothing and rides an armadillo. However much the panicking writer jams his spurs into the armadillo's flanks, the leathery little beast doesn't feel a thing and just trots along at a lazy pace until, well, you don't need the details but the daydream ends as you'd hope, with me placing a size 10 on the writer's chest and posing for the camera while swigging manfully from my magnum.

But I wouldn't hunt this novelist. He is fun to be with, he oozes human sympathy, and he wields words with a precision that I can only envy.

We were in the pub. How we got there is a story that would take too long to tell. You could ask the novelist if you liked, but frankly I wouldn't advise it. He makes his living out of telling fibs. I'm afraid you'll have to take it as a given, just as you take it as a given that Monday was the Queen's birthday, which it wasn't. Apparently she was spawned in April, emerging fully formed in a tiara and with one gloved hand waving to the midwife. Or so the novelist told me.

Anyway, it was one of those out-of-date pubs that still survive in Lyttelton to cater to the rougher end of the trading spectrum, the thirst-racked mariners and smoke-raddled locals who like their carpet squelchy. The place was packed. At one end stood the cause of the packedness – two doleful-looking muso's and one undoleful-looking singer. The singer was my sort of singer, a Piaf, only substantially more substantial than Piaf. But just like Piaf she sings defiance, belting out the old favourites in a voice as rich as rum. And again just like Piaf, this woman has known no shortage of tragedy in her life, and you could hear it in the voice. No one could achieve that richness, that zest, that irony, that sky-challenging relish, who had not spent a considerable time being dangled upside down over the big black pit of despair that stinks like J. K. Baxter's armpits.

I explained all this to the novelist and he thought a bit, then said that if it wasn't for misery life would be miserable. I said I thought that was a good line. He made me promise not to steal it for a column. I promised, and furthermore I let him know that I was a man of my word. What I didn't let him know is that my word is hypocrisy.

I wasn't the only one thrilling to this singer. As she bashed out 'Ghost Riders', 'Green Door' and a string of other tunes so familiar they are part of the fabric of every head, she released in me and a hundred others a wellspring of disinhibition that found ugly but honest ways of expressing itself. Some danced, some sang, some gawped, and one woman felt an urge that she did not resist to shout at me about the many and splendid virtues of her cat. And in the far corner of the bar, between the fruit machines and the door, a bunch of men had a fight.

There was lots of swearing and barging and forearms across throats and chests puffed up like cockerels, but nothing of the take-that-you-bounder freely swung and virtuous fist. Indeed it wasn't easy in the hubbub to distinguish the fight from the dancing and the singing and the whole delightful pell-mell.

And it was then that I had my momentary epiphany, my epiph. Here it was, the lot, in the present tense. All human life was here, burdened with a freight of bad yesterdays but with no thought to the possibilities of a bad tomorrow. People would be going to work the next day with throats like Iraq and heads like the finale of the '1812', but who cared? Tomorrow was a foreign country we would never visit. And who gave a fig for the gradual sagging of skin, or the rebuffs of children or the blown head gasket or the pimpled bum? Who cared that the Queen had chosen to celebrate her unbirthday by dubbing Mr Holmes for services to music? No thought to anything but now, and plucking the strong flower of pleasure from the perilous slopes of the abyss, as Baxter more or less put it.

I was epiphed. My face must have given me away.

'What's up?' said the novelist.

'I'm epiphed,' I said.

The novelist smiled and said, 'Yeph, me too.'

Stuff love

Love and trust, you can keep them. Particularly love. I've had it with love.

There you are washed up on the blank beach of middle age like an empty Fanta bottle, discarded, turning brittle in the sun, ignored by the cackle-throated gulls, essentially an ex-thing, a husk, a was, when in sweeps the spring tide of love and lifts you off the beach and, whoa, suddenly you're flinging about like a teenage Fanta bottle, full of fizz and zest and cruel delusion. Well, stuff that. I'm not falling for it again. I'm going to buy myself an anchor and cling limpet-like to the beach for ever until, well, until the next spring tide rolls in and the whole caboodle runs its ghastly little up and down course again.

And as for trust, well, I'll get to that in a minute.

Love? Ha. And that's a ha with a curled lip and an ironic tone that it's tricky to convey on paper. You should see how hard I'm hitting the keys. Fair whacking them, I am. Like that. And that.

I didn't love the Subaru. Oh no. We were just friends. Familiar. Comfortable. Easy. 'Oh hello,' I'd say each morning, 'you still here? Good.' And off we'd putter to the grog shop for a drop of breakfast and everything was dandy. Nothing to upset the dreary round of routine; time passing as time does. Then suddenly, folly. Sheer lunatic folly. I fell for, well, I can't bring myself to type the name. Let's just say a car, a particular car. My tired flesh surged and pulsed with want. Primal stuff. Want want want. Want that retractable roof. Want that remote control key fob. Want those cupholders, that plethora of compartments for keeping things in, those fog lamps, those, God help me, bull bars.

Bull bars? Ha, again. I know I'm saying ha a lot, but that's because ha's exactly right. If these bull bars met a bull, they'd shrivel and crumple before you could say pretentious simulacrum of bogus masculinity. They're lamb bars, weasel bars, supermarket-shopping-trolley bars.

But I bought them. Oh yes, I shelled out the money that I love, to run my vein-mapped hands over them, to fondle their chromium curves. I was deaf, dumb, blind, stupid with love. Love is wilful. Love is obtuse. Love whisks you out of the top set – 'gifted' is what they call the clever ones, these days, gifted, ha – and dumps you in the intensive care remedial class alongside the boneheads and the thumb-suckers. And yet, you just don't care.

I gave the Subaru away. For zilch. For a beer. Three hundred thousand kilometres it had trundled with me in its belly and nary a whimper. It was merely and honorably functional, dependable, a Dobbin of the road, a plodder, and I gave it away like an empty Fanta bottle to Dave. Dave who's just passed his driving test. 'Here you are, son,' I said, '1800cc of turbocharged reliable freedom,' and he said ta and took it straight to the carwash as I never once did, never once, and then he parked it where I can see it from my window now, gleaming and sneering, my ex.

And in its stead, in place of old dependable, I've got this gadget-laden… thing. I'm exactly like that nonagenarian tetrazillionaire from

Kansas who, when only a stumble short of the eternal landfill, married a twenty-year-old strippeuse with implants.

Well, the old fool's dead now and so is love, my love. Or rather not dead, but transmuted into a smouldering hatred, rich as a diesel exhaust. I've only got to catch sight of those lamb bars, that high-mounted brake light, I've only got to hear the pre-pubertal beep beep beep the thing emits when it goes backwards, to seethe with loathing, disgust, disgust at self. Because that's what this car represents, of course, an abject lapse of self-awareness. 'This above all,' said whoever it was in Shakespeare, 'to thine own self be true, and it must follow, as the night the day, thou canst not then be false to any man.' Easy to say, and even easier to ignore.

So, yesterday I decided to lance the boil of love gone sour. I went to trade the thing in after less than a month. Round the ghastly caryards of Moorhouse Avenue I went, which is exactly like snorkelling with sharks. But now I knew what I was looking for. My only criterion was that I mustn't love the thing. If my heart gave a little lurch at the sight of a car, I just walked on by. And I found what I wanted, a car so dull it's effectively invisible, a car so utilitarian and square that it looks more like a box than a box does.

The deal should happen tomorrow, if, that is, I can trust the dealer. Which reminds me, I said I'd anatomise trust. Well, that's a doddle. Trust? Same as love. Ha.

Where do you go to?

Sleep's good, especially at Christmas, but going to sleep is better. I know nothing more delicious than sliding from wake into sleep. It's a letting go, a submission. You let slip the constructed self, the armour that you don each day to fight the world. As you fall asleep it slithers off as softly as a dress of silk. Even the hardest gang-man, the most shaven-headed, sex-tongued, greed-driven, hate-brimming, finger-jabbing, gun-stroking bully boy slides into softness each night, vulnerable as his own fraught psyche.

It's the journey into utter privacy, the time of most alone, like a hermit withdrawing deep into the darkness of the cave. And in the darkness up swims sleep. It's the oldest daily miracle.

How does it happen? How does the thug go to sleep? How do you? Do you count sheep? I doubt it. I have never met anyone who counts sheep. The conscious act of counting defies the rise of the mind that dreams.

I play cricket. Or rather every night I replay a little bit of cricket, a single moment that happened twenty years ago. I know exactly where the game was played. I can see the ground, the hedges that surround it, the long grass inside them, then the close-cut turf of the outfield half bleached by the summer, the fresher green of the square, the mower's stripes, the pitch itself. Lying in bed, I can feel the sun of twenty summers ago on my forearms.

I am batting. A young man runs in to bowl. His shirt is flapping. He leaps at the crease and bowls. The ball is overpitched, a half-volley, juicy as a summer plum. The air is spangle-bright. I can see the gold lettering on the ball, the raised stitches of the seam. I lean forward, drawn to the ball with a sort of midsummer ease. My movement has the pace of flowing honey. Like honey it is sweet and simple. Body and bat are one.

The sound of the ball in the bat's heart is as rich as a church bell. No jarring. No sense of impact. It is like a caress, a channelling of affection, and the ball's direction simply reverses. The ball has come to me and then it has gone away from me as I have desired that it should. I haven't hit the ball, I have expressed it. It feels as natural and as languid as a dog's stretch, as a river's flow.

At a speed that surprises me the ball scuds across the turf as straight as the hand of a clock. Mid-off makes a hopeless dive at it. His floundering clumsiness occupies a different realm to the progress of the ball from my bat to the field's far edge.

I take a stride or two up the pitch, knowing I've no need to run but doing so for form's sake. The ball's speed, its impetus, is mine. I am attached to it as it travels. It owes its movement to me. Look, I did that.

Forty, fifty, sixty yards away now, and it is still running on the fuel I fed it through the simple arc and flow of my body and my bat. It crosses the boundary and plunges into the long and withered grass of summer, where it comes to rest, held by a mesh of tangled stems that binds it like a cradle. It's made a nest, like a small animal. I sent it there. And in my mind I join it there, in its nest of long grasses.

Its arrival upsets a tiny metropolis. It's the meteor that flattens New York. Ants, spiders, grasshoppers, a thousand insects I can't name, scurry for safety in the mulch of spent vegetation, frantic for the darkness and the rich moist soil. The ball waits. In my head I wait with it, waiting for the disturbance to subside in this miniature jungle.

Slowly peace returns. The spindly spider resumes its high-stepping progress through the stems, its arched legs as frail as its own gossamer. Ants go back to their co-operative business. Mites, woodlice and a million microscopic creatures re-emerge to scout and fossick through their tiny world. And I am among them, not moving, just seeing and being there, where no one cares or matters, where death is common and ordinary and regenerative and where no cricket scores ever penetrate, where no words are written, where no words exist, but where the endless web of brief and interdependent lives goes on going on. I sink into it. And as I sink the other self rises, the night-time self that can go anywhere with its strange alternative logic. I am asleep. Happy Christmas.